MW01609823

FROM *Heart* TO *Hand*

The Lost Art of a Written Letter

KRISTIN HORVATH

BALBOA.
PRESS
A DIVISION OF HAY HOUSE

Balboa Press books may be ordered through booksellers or by contacting:

Balboa Press
A Division of Hay House
1663 Liberty Drive
Bloomington, IN 47403
www.balboapress.com
1 (877) 407-4847

Because of the dynamic nature of the Internet, any web addresses or
links contained in this book may have changed since publication and
may no longer be valid. The views expressed in this work are solely those
of the author and do not necessarily reflect the views of the publisher,
and the publisher hereby disclaims any responsibility for them.

The author of this book does not dispense medical advice or prescribe the use
of any technique as a form of treatment for physical, emotional, or medical
problems without the advice of a physician, either directly or indirectly. The
intent of the author is only to offer information of a general nature to help
you in your quest for emotional and spiritual well-being. In the event you use
any of the information in this book for yourself, which is your constitutional
right, the author and the publisher assume no responsibility for your actions.

Any people depicted in stock imagery provided by Thinkstock are
models, and such images are being used for illustrative purposes only.
Certain stock imagery © Thinkstock.

Print information available on the last page.

ISBN: 978-1-5043-5867-5 (sc)
ISBN: 978-1-5043-5866-8 (hc)
ISBN: 978-1-5043-5869-9 (e)

Library of Congress Control Number: 2016908449

Balboa Press rev. date: 07/21/2016

To my mother, Shirley Horvath, who taught
me how to write my first letter.
To my son, Christopher, who listened to me
along the way and inspires me every day.

"Everything in life comes back to one thing: the heart. Kristin does an amazing job extracting the beauty of each letter - making it relevant to the digital life today. Why read this book? It reminds you of what life is all about, what we all continue to search for everyday: Love."
– Hailey Yatros, author: *The Millennial Makeover.*

Contents

Acknowledgments

Dear Friends,

This book is for all of you who have ever written a letter, thought recently about writing a letter and for all of you who continue to still write letters to this day. This book is for all of you who have a passion and dream inside of you that wants to come out and be shared with the world. This book is for my family, immediate and extended who have allowed me to be my authentic self on my life's journey. For my brother Rob, being the oldest has come with a lot of responsibility. I can't thank you enough for the understanding you always show and for your continued support. For my brother Paul, who came up with and gave me the beautiful title for this book one night as we were doing one of our favorite things together, sitting outside by the fire, thank you. For my sister Kathryn, whose creative genius amazes and inspires me in so many ways, thank you. To my son Christopher, it is the letters I write to you that are my favorite and the love I have for you that fills my heart the most. To all of the friends who have wholeheartedly supported me on my journey at any point along the way. To Karen Will Rogers who opened her home to me in Nashville, for all we have been through together in the two years I have been here and for taking and also editing all the beautiful pictures that have been included in this book, thank you my friend. To my parents, Robert and Shirley Horvath, for every bit of love and support you provided all of us with and for all that you instilled in us. Dad, I feel you with me every day and mom; I can't wait to hand you the first copy of this book and to see the smile on your face. I want to say thank you, thank you, thank you to anyone whom I ever sent a letter to because without those letters I wouldn't have this, my first book. My heart is filled with love, gratitude and great appreciation.

From My Heart and Hand to Yours,
Kristin A. Horwath

Introduction

Is there someone who has been on your mind lately? Do you remember the days when this would happen and, instead of picking up the phone to make a long-distance call, you would pull out some stationery and pen, sit, and take the time to write him or her a letter? There was almost something calming and spiritual about this process—sealing the envelope, picking out a stamp, walking down to the mailbox, and putting up the red flag as your letter sat there waiting for the mailman to pick it up and get it to its intended destination.

Do you remember when you would open the mailbox at the end of what seemed to be a very long day and, among the junk and bills, find it, an envelope addressed to you with the return address label actually from a friend? When was the last time you received a letter? When was the last time you wrote a missive? Undoubtedly writing letters has become a lost art, but hopefully after reading this, you will be inspired to help in the revitalization of the lost art of a written letter.

What you are about to read are honest, authentic, and sometimes even embarrassing, but always heartfelt, letters of gratitude I have written to people who have inspired me or helped me, thanking them for the help or inspiration they provided in my life. If you enjoy love, laughter, and sentimental stories that show complete vulnerability, you will enjoy sinking your teeth into this work, and you might end up writing a letter to someone you have been meaning to catch up with.

Chapter 1
Family Ties

A Mother-Son Bond: I Love This Kid

Dear Christopher,

I have held on to the thoughts of this letter in my heart for quite some time, waiting for that right moment to share those feelings with you, and there is no better time than on your graduation from film school. Sometimes I don't even know where to begin, as my eyes well up with tears with all the thoughts I have about you as my son.

To be a parent—to be your parent—has filled me with a love that even I have a hard time finding the words to describe, but one thing I do know is how much I love being your mother. Having held your hand along the way—as you were growing up and then letting go so you could find your own path—has been an incredible experience to be a part of. You were such a good kid, an easygoing child, and a philosophical young man who, in my eyes, even though you might not have always seen it, has understood his life. And because of this, deep down you understand others so well, and the benefits you will have in life because of this will be endless. My life has been blessed since the moment you entered this world. You are a blessing for whom I will give thanks every day for the rest of my life.

It is truly inspirational to watch you find yourself over the past many years of your young adulthood, to watch you find what you love to do, and to watch you go through the whole process of learning how to do it. It has moved me every day. I know at times it might have felt like a long road to get where you are today, but the most important thing for you to know and remember about the path you have gone down is how many people love you and support you. We would do whatever we could to help you fulfill your passions in life. I knew if there were nothing else I could give you, I could always provide you with an overabundant amount of love. I knew I could surround you with people who love you just as much as I do. And as a result, you have truly been blessed with lots of love. Nanny and Pappy, your aunts and uncles, great-aunts and great-uncles who just adore you, your cousins, and your friends and mine all love you because their love comes from the deepest, truest parts of their hearts, not because of their relationship to me. It's all for you.

As a parent, you question decisions you make at times. You always want to give your child (or your children) moments and things they can take away from. Despite what others might have said about my decision to live at home and raise you with Nanny and Pappy, I wouldn't change that for the world. Because of everything it gave you, it also gave back to me tenfold! The list of monetary things you had because of that decision is endless; however, it was so much more than that as to why I made that choice. It was because of the relationship it gave you with your nanny and pappy. Those memories and that bond can never be broken, not even in death.

You know, I do believe Pappy is here in spirit. He's been guiding and reminding you of all the important things he taught you, especially about having a great work ethic. I see so many qualities of him in you, and I absolutely love it. I will say he did spoil you a bit too much, but you continue to learn from the life he gave you. He loved you more than anything. I know I wouldn't change the decision I made or the incredible relationship you had with your pappy and still have with your nanny, not for anything in the world.

You've had a different life from most. You've had to learn some tough lessons at a young age, but learn you did. You have learned from the life that has been given to you, and you have grown because of those lessons. You have been understanding toward it, and this has created your strengths. It's given you tremendous character, and I am so proud of you.

These twenty-three years have all gone by so quickly. Because of the great memories we have created together, there is so much I miss about having you here. Having you has been the best journey I have ever been on, and I wouldn't trade it for anything in the world.

I love you. I am so proud of you. I will always support you as best I can and in any way!

With a love and bond from my whole heart and soul,
Mom

★ ★ ★

Sometimes the best thank-you that one can ever receive is the least-expected one. I was lucky enough to spend New Year's Eve with my son that year. After we returned home, we walked into the kitchen.

He stopped, looked at me, and said, "You know, Mom, I really just wanted to thank you for all you have ever done for me."

I looked at him, nodded, and said, "I know." My eyes welled up with tears.

He put his arms around me and said, "No, really. Thank you, Mom."

We just stood there and hugged each other tightly. My eyes still well up with tears thinking about that beautiful moment we shared that day. It was even more special, as he was moving to Los Angeles the very next day to pursue his dreams and passions.

★ ★ ★

Enlightenment

Dear Uncle Craig and Aunt Gloria,

I wanted to take the time to thank you for all the books you have sent to me and, more importantly, for opening my eyes, heart, and mind to such wonderful ways of looking at life and the world we live in. I can't express enough what a great impact each and every book has had on me in its own way. Whether it's learning to be more positive with our energy and thoughts, learning how to cleanse situations (my own or others), realizing I am my own soul mate (something I think I have always known), or just gaining knowledge about others' lives, many of whom I never knew anything about. I always say that knowledge is power. And for all of this, I thank you.

But more importantly than the books and DVDs you have sent me, I am thankful for the interest you have always taken in me and the guidance you have shown me along the way. For this and more I am very grateful. I am enjoying this recent journey that you have opened me up to, and I can't wait to see where it takes me so I can share it with you along the way. Somehow I have the feeling you already know where I am going and where this journey is leading me, and that thought alone gives me great comfort. I know you would never lead me down a path I wasn't meant to be on. What I love even more is sharing this journey with both of you, as well as the honest, heartfelt joy you impart with me when you see me have one of those aha moments about my life.

So again—and I can't say it enough—thank you! I am truly grateful to have the both of you in my life.

Peace, love, and happiness,
Kristin

★ ★ ★

This letter was the first I wrote in my efforts to revitalize the lost art of a personalized handwritten letter. I intentionally chose my Aunt Gloria and Uncle Craig as recipients. They are such huge supporters of my efforts to follow my passions and find my life purpose. It was very important for me to set my intention and give thanks and thoughts of gratitude to the two people I consider to be my own personal spiritual gurus. They are both such a big part of my life, and I knew I had to include them in the initial part of this journey.

Just a few months ago, my aunt suggested a new box set for me, Louise Hay's *You Can Heal Your Life.*

I said, "Okay, I will go order it right now."

I always knew that random books that showed up unexpectedly on my doorstep were from either Craig or Gloria. So when they would recommend a book to me, I didn't ask any questions. I always just ordered it and read it. It was always what I needed to read right at that moment in my life. This book and DVD by Louise Hay was no exception. To date, *You Can Heal Your Life* has, by far, had the biggest impact in my life. I could probably write a whole book about how learning to love myself, forgiving myself and others, doing affirmations, and more has made me feel. This book opened me up to look at life in a more beautiful, positive way than I ever had before. It is wonderful when family members get you and you know that they will never lead you astray and always support you. Once you fully understand that, you also know that they want nothing but good things for you.

Their support gives me the confidence to know that I can create anything I want. It is an amazing relationship I have with Craig and Gloria. I am a better person because they are in my life. I could have written a hundred letters to my aunt Gloria and uncle Craig over the past several years, telling them how grateful I am for them, and a hundred letters wouldn't have been enough thanks for all the support they continue to show me.

I do want to say the first book Craig sent to me will, by far, always be my favorite. It was shortly after I had walked away from my human resources career to follow my passion for cooking and had enrolled in culinary school. Lo and behold in my mailbox one day, the best of all the best culinary books that was ever written, Larousse's *Gastronomique*, arrived. This was an absolute culinary masterpiece. Craig knew I had to have it, and so it was.

★ ★ ★

A Cousin's Love

Dear Jody,

Happy New Year to you, Eric, Benjamin, and Morgan! I hope your Christmas holiday was wonderful and Eric's dad is recovering well, but more importantly, I trust that you guys got some time away to share together as a family. I have been thinking of you since your last e-mail to me, updating me of your new adventure for 2011, and I wanted to say how excited I am for you. I think you will do great as a life coach, and I can speak from experience on that. To this day I am very thankful for some of those little changes you suggested I make in my life. I literally sleep better because of it.

I think that following your passions is so important, and I am so glad to hear that this is part of your training with teenage girls. As a woman now in my forties, I am a firm believer that it is never too late to follow those passions you may have had as a child or young adult, and that is why I am taking those horseback riding lessons, buying a new camera, and writing more. I've had a passion for these things over so many years, and I never did anything about until now, so I think it's great that you're helping young women learn earlier than I did about how to follow your passions.

I can't wait to hear how your women's forum goes this month and some of the exciting things you will be discussing. I wish you the best of luck with all of this. It is so exciting, and I can't wait to hear about your journey along the way.

I also wanted to take a second to thank you for being such a loving cousin. I am extremely grateful for these few close relationships I have with family, and I just wanted you to know how much I appreciate you as a part of my life. Here is to a very blessed 2011 for us all.

Love you dearly,
Kristin

★ ★ ★

Jody and I are only three weeks apart in age and have been very close our whole lives. Every summer growing up, we would take turns spending a week at a time going to each other's homes. This was like camp to us. It became our family tradition, something we looked forward to every year.

Now we laugh, remembering all the different things that would happen during those magical weeks we would spend growing up with each other. I have been blessed with a big family, and I am even more fortunate to have such lovely relationships with so many of my cousins, aunts, and uncles that I am truly grateful for. Even though we have aged, our own families have grown, our paths have gone in different directions, and we have experienced losses of loved ones, I love that we make a point to get together a couple times a year to still enjoy each other's company. We make the effort to stay connected because of the love we have for each other, and there is nothing better than just that, love between families.

★ ★ ★

A Diamond Is Forever: Welcome to the Family

Dear Jimmy,

Let me start off by saying congratulations and welcome to the family. I couldn't be more excited for you and Erin during this time of your lives, and I am thrilled you will soon be my cousin-in-law. I wish I had some great words of wisdom for you, but in all honesty, after watching your relationship over the past five years, I think you guys will be more than fine. I see you two are compatible, you have respect for each other, you support each other, you have love and friendship between you, and you have a ton of fun with each other. And because of all this, I know you are the perfect person for my cousin, who is very dear to me.

As I said to Erin last night, I can't wait to watch you guys go on this journey together. I am truly happy for the both of you! Congratulations again, Jimmy.

Love you, buddy,
Kristin

★ ★ ★

My cousin Erin and I have been close since the day she was born, and to this day, we continue to talk and check in with each other about once a month. Wherever we go together, people always ask if we are sisters, which I love because she is more like the little sister I never had. I have always been protective of her, supportive of her wherever she has been in her life with what she is doing, and proud of her. I love so much the memories of all the trips that Erin and I have taken together, including visiting her wherever she has lived—from Marquette, Michigan (where

9

she went to college) to all my visits out to Colorado—to getting together when she comes to town, eating her mom's famous lasagna, drinking her dad's homemade wine, and always having incredible conversations about life. I am truly excited for her and Jimmy, and I am full of love for the both of them.

★ ★ ★

Friends Are Family Too

Dear Aunt Rose,

I wanted to take a minute to send you this letter to let you know I have been thinking of you for the past several months. I was so sad to hear that Uncle John had passed away, and my prayers and thoughts have been with you. I also want to share a little story with you that I hope helps you find some comfort with all the emotions I can only imagine you have been going through.

Eight and a half years ago, when my dad was in the hospital, having just been diagnosed with pancreatic cancer, you and Uncle John sent him some books to read with a beautiful card. It simply read, "Dear Bob, Thinking of you. Thought you might enjoy the enclosed. We hope you are home soon. Love and God bless, John and Rose."

The card had pictures of butterflies on it with a beautiful gold edging around it. The perfect printing on the inside, stating those words I know my father needed to hear at that moment in the last few days of his life, still fills me today with such a warmth every time I hold this card in my hands. For reasons unknown to me at the time, but ones I have completely embraced and come to understand over the past few years, I kept this card. I can't tell you how many times I have pulled it out and read it, looked at it, held it in my hands, and ran my fingers over it. I would pull out the card when I missed my dad, and I wanted to feel connected to him like Uncle John and my dad were connected with each other in their lifelong friendship. They had a bond with each other that was so admirable. One could only be blessed to have a friendship like they had.

I know they are together now, having a good time. I know they are watching over us and smiling down on us. And this thought fills my heart with love. Aunt Rose, we were truly blessed to have them in our lives. Now as an adult, I understand what a true friendship is, more so than I have ever known in my life. I recognize what it is to unconditionally love your friends, and this is because of the absolute love of a friendship that my dad and your husband shared with each other for so many years. I love that I am still learning things from my father now, even though he has been gone for over eight years, and I love that I can still feel him with me.

I was going through my photos albums the other day and came across this picture that was taken of the five of us: you, me, Uncle John, my mom, and my dad. I thought you would enjoy having a copy of it. I always loved the visits, and as you can see from this picture, I would always find a way to put myself right in the center of it all. I appreciated listening to the stories that were shared all the way back to their school days together and then so many years of friendship moving forward. It still makes me smile to think of them all. My parents' relationship with the two of you taught me family is beyond the bloodline and friends are family too.

My thoughts and prayers are with you, Aunt Rose.

With a heart full of love,
Kristin

* * *

Uncle John and Aunt Rose have always been just that to me, my aunt and uncle. My dad met John when they were in high school together at Catholic Central, and both went to college at the University of Detroit, where I subsequently received my first two degrees as well. This friendship spanned over sixty years with a million stories and memories and even more love that came along with it. I would watch their house when they went out of town and take care of their cat. And I would pop in to visit every now and again when I was in high school because they lived right around the corner. It was an incredible friendship in my eyes and even more so to me when I reflect upon it today because they were always just family to me. And that says a lot because, no matter where they come from, family is everything.

Chapter 2
Friends

We couldn't get through life without our friends. I have always thought and said that friends come into your life for a reason a season or a lifetime, and in this chapter you will see just that.

★ ★ ★

Coworker Turned Confidant Turned Lifelong Friend

My dear friend Erin,

It has been a while since we have seen each other, but I think of you often, and I miss you dearly. I just wanted to drop you a quick little note to let you know how dear you still are to me, and to wish you a Happy New Year. You know, during these specific times of remembrance, such as New Year's, I become very reflective and thankful for all the things I have, have had, and will have in my life, and I am extremely grateful for my friends. Even though we have not connected as much as I have thought of you or wanted to, I still think of you as a very dear friend in my life. You were there for me in an extraordinary time of pain and grief in my life through the diagnosis and passing of my father. And because of your kind heart that you showed to me during that time, I will forever be bonded to our friendship.

Even if we go months without talking or years without seeing each other, I consider you one of the dearest friends I have had in my life, and I just wanted to share that with you and let you know how you are always in my thoughts and prayers. Even now when things get tough and crazy, personally and professionally, I sometimes stop and just think of how, during those days of working together, when things got crazy, we could trust each other (which is hard to find these days) and laugh together (and no one could laugh and cry at the same time like you). And we knew somehow we would get through it.

In so many ways I wish we would have never had most of those horrible days, but they formed part of who I am and where I am with life today. And more importantly, without them, I wouldn't have met you. So because of that, I know everything has its reasons. I thank you for being there with all we went through so many years ago and the timeless friendship I feel because of it. I love you and miss you.

Wishing you a lifetime of great friendships,
Kristin

★ ★ ★

Even though it took more than a year after I sent my letter, Erin and I finally got together. When I see my friend Erin, this is what friendship is all about, picking up right where you left off as if no time has passed at all. We talked nonstop for over four hours, and we probably could have sat there for four more. She is just so wise and such a great mother, and she is so honest and true to herself and her life with her husband and her sons. She is just an amazing woman, and I am so proud to call her a dear friend.

To this day, when I think of her, I love that I know in my heart how she will always be a dear friend to me, no matter how much time goes between our conversations and our visits with each other. For this simple reason she is such a good person or, as I like to say, a good egg. One can only be blessed to have such a good friend in his or her life.

Whenever Erin and I talk, we laugh the whole time. We talk about the kids and common friends, and we get caught up on where we are in our lives. And even though our lives are on different paths, we have always stayed connected to each other. Erin and I both say that we know circumstances in our lives have changed, but over the past decade, our friendship has done nothing but grow. It continues to grow out of love every time we talk.

I especially love when we talk about the kids, and because of our children's age differences, Erin really listens to the experiences I have been through and takes them to heart. And I just chuckle at the stories that take me back to when my son was their ages. I love the things she has to say about her personal experiences of being a mother and wife and not losing herself along the way as well. She has such a wisdom into her life's purpose from her own events of losing her father at the age of five. It is an incredible thing for me to hear her talk about.

I also love talking with Erin about friendship: the friends we've had for years, the new friends we've had come into our lives, and the friends we've had to let go of because there were just no more commonalities there. I love when we talk about how important it is to follow your heart with all the relationships in your life and know when they are right and observe when they are not. This is truly a friendship that has been built from a place of love, and there is no better friendship to have than the one I have with Erin.

★ ★ ★

Second Chances: Everything Always Works Out the Way It Was Meant To

Dear Patrick,

I wanted to take just a few minutes to say thank you for giving me the opportunity I had passed on so many years ago, that is, allowing myself to let you fully into my life. Without that opportunity, I would have always wondered what could have been with you. And now I know, and it is the best feeling in the world to not have to wonder "what if" about something. As hard as it has been for the past six months to get over my thoughts of you that have been built up for the past twenty-plus years (good, bad, and indifferent), I can say everything does have its reasons for happening the way they do. I am honestly grateful for most of the time we had together. Sometimes it's just nice having someone there.

I am sorry for how it all ended, and unfortunately we cannot change that. This may not sound or feel like a traditional thank-you letter, but I am truly thankful for all the experiences I had with you. I just wanted you to know. I wish you the best in your life, Patrick.

God bless,
Kristin

★ ★ ★

I met Patrick for the first time at my cousin's wedding, I believe, in 1990. He was my cousin's husband's identical twin brother, and we became fast friends. We wrote letters back and forth, called one another over the years, and visited each other, but we just never seemed to be on the same page at the same time.

So in 2009, almost twenty years after we first met, the opportunity presented itself, and we took a chance on something I thought I had missed out on. Everything has its reasons for working out the way they do, and there are no hard feelings left between us. Patrick did call me about a month or so after he received this letter and thanked me for it.

A few times a year, we share some text messages back and forth, just checking in to see how each other is doing and wishing one another other well. I do believe in second chances, and I am still glad to this day that I got this opportunity because it is better to have loved, learned, and lost than never having the opportunity to love at all.

★ ★ ★

The letters I have included in this book are honest thoughts that come straight from the heart and how I was feeling at the time they were written. As I stated at the beginning of this chapter, friends come into your life for a reason, a season, or a lifetime. The same friend can also come in and out of your life at many different points. Just because he or she might not be a part of your life right at this moment doesn't mean that the words written to him or her weren't true. Sometimes friends just lose their commonalities with each other, and there is nothing left beyond those similarities. It doesn't make anyone right or wrong. It just makes it what it is, beautiful moments that are now memories, knowing all is forgiven.

Sorority Sisters: Truly Grateful for the Friendship That Had Several Seasons

Dear Bridgett,

When I think of our friendship, many thoughts come to the forefront of my mind, but most of all, I love the uniqueness in our relationship the most, the complete understanding of who we are as individuals and friends. You are a very giving person not only of great little gifts but of your time, energies, thoughts, and, most importantly, kindness. We have had some meetings of the mind in our friendship, along with some little battles, but the most important thing in our friendship is how honest we can be with each other. It is something I appreciate so much, along with the delicacy, gentleness, and laughter that comes with it. I truly want nothing but the best for you in life, along with your dreams, thoughts, and desires to come true for you. You can have all of these things just by opening up and letting down the walls, and this will allow you to be able to give all the love you have in your heart. And you have a lot of that. Sometimes we just have to breathe through the hard times and believe in the greatness that is ahead for both of us. I am forever thankful and grateful that I met you during our college sorority days. It is the best thing that the Tri Sigma community could have ever given me.

One thing I absolutely love about you—probably because others have such a hard time being able to do this because of their own fears and lack of understanding about the people in their lives—is your ability and willingness to unite such eclectic groups of people together. I have met many wonderful people through you. I have gained some great acquaintances and some even more lovely friendships that I would not have had other than you bringing people together. This is such an incredible part of your strong character and shows how truly secure you are within yourself. Believe me when I say I have those friends in my life who keep their groups of friends very separate because of their own fears, and you love them in spite of it.

Years had gone by before we reconnected after college, and when we finally did, it was like no time had passed at all. I knew right then and there what a good soul you were and what a wonderful spirit you have. I am truly blessed to call you a friend. I adore and love you from the bottom of my heart. I hope you know how much I do cherish our friendship.

From my heart to yours, with Sigma love and mine,

Kristin

When We Spell Our Names the Same, We Were Bound to Be Friends

My dear friend Kristin,

I am writing this letter to you to let you know how grateful I am for our friendship. I know we don't talk as much as we used to, but I want you to realize that it doesn't mean I am not thinking of you. In fact I do, and I am always wishing complete happiness for you and love with all you do and have. My heart fills with the warmth of joy when I think of the timeline of our friendship. All relationships change as one's life adapts over the years, and when I think of our relationship, I believe there is strength and love to our friendship that is as strong today as it has ever been. I know, as those big moments still come to us in our lives, the list is short as to whom I would share those with, and you are at the absolute top of that list. I also know, if I need an honest opinion on any topic, I can get that from you, and I think that your honesty might be one of the things I love about you most. That is a quality hard to find in people today, and it says a lot about your character.

I hope you and Jay had a great Christmas with your family as well as a wonderful New Year. Give my best to both Jay and Campbell, and I hope you guys are surviving this winter down there.

I thank you for our friendship. I miss you and love you.

Kristin

★ ★ ★

Kristin is a friend whom I love very much, and I will honestly admit that I do miss a part of our single days together, but I know I am blessed to have all the years together we've had. We met in Chicago in the early nineties when we were there on business, attending a seminar. We have never lived in the same city, and through most of our friendship, we lived in different states, but we visited each other all the time and had many years of single girl weekends together.

Even better, Kristin was my friend whom I could talk sports with. Most of our time together was spent at some sporting event, whether it was the Wabash versus Depaw football game every November for almost a decade, a March Madness basketball game, or a major league baseball game. Whatever state we were in and whenever season it was, we went to several sporting events together. Those are the memories I love the most.

Kristin is married now to a wonderful man and has had her first beautiful miracle, a little baby girl. She has primarily taught me that you don't have to let go of a friendship because life has changed. We can still pick up the phone, talk, and pick up right where we left off from, having the feeling as if it were yesterday that we spoke. And that is a wonderful feeling, especially when we need each other in moments of uncertainty or loss in our lives that we are going through, like last year when her beautiful dog Kallie, whom she had rescued so many years before, wasn't going to make it another day. I was blessed to be able to say my good-byes and tell Kallie that her Aunt Kristin loved her. When I would visit Kristin, I always had one day scheduled where Kristin would go to work and Kallie and I would get to hang out, just the two of us, and we'd go for long walks and cuddles on the couch. Yes, my friend's pets call me Aunt Kristin too, and Kallie was one of my favorites.

This is one of my friendships where I am so very thankful for technology. There is nothing I love more than receiving pictures of Kristin's daughter Colby or the FaceTime phone calls, watching her growing so much. This is priceless to me since we live so far away from each other.

Even though a tinge of me misses our single friendship we shared together for so many years, to see a friend have everything in her life that she had once just dreamed about—a home, a wonderful husband, and children of her own—fills me with even more love for our friendship. I also want to say that Kristin's wedding was probably one of the most beautiful ceremonies I have been a part of. Being there with her the morning of her wedding was such a special moment in our friendship. Being able to give her a rosary my father had given to me as something borrowed and something blue, knowing the rosary was on loan so she could give it back to me on my wedding day, is how special Kristin's friendship is to me.

★ ★ ★

The Horse Whisperer: Fulfilling a Childhood Dream

Dear Kerrin,

I just want to take a second to thank you for helping me fulfill a childhood dream of mine, teaching me how to saddle up and properly ride a horse. I also want to thank you for your patience with me. I know I haven't caught on as quickly as others do. I know I don't have the form and abilities that others do. I know it's easy to make fun of me (as I do of myself), but I want you to know how much I love coming out for my lessons. To have the ability to do something you have always wanted to do is amazing, and without you guiding me along the way, especially when I feel I have two left hands and legs. I wouldn't be able to do it. I am getting there slowly but surely, and so is my comfort level.

I am truly grateful for your time and understanding during my lessons, and I look forward to getting better and more comfortable and just maybe taking a jump or two someday. These lessons have done so much for me. It's my therapy in so many ways. It has continued to teach me to pursue my passions and the things I love and to never let go of those interests and make excuses for not doing them. I'm to just put one foot in front of the other to find my way toward the things I love.

I have learned so much from you, not only about horses but also about life. It's never too late, and you're never too old to accomplish the things you have always wanted to. Thanks again for your time, energy, and efforts with me. I am so grateful for it.

Thank you again,
Kristin

★ ★ ★

This was more than a childhood dream of mine that I was fulfilling. I loved horses so much when I was a kid. I know now horses were probably the first thing I was passionate about, that and wanting to learn how to cook from watching my mom making dinner for us every night. Every time we went to the Ben Franklin, I would beg my mom to let me get a little horse figurine, whether it was metal or plastic. Whatever material it was made of, I didn't care. I just wanted a collection of horses.

About two years ago, I packed up those miniature horses and took them to the local Goodwill. I felt it was time for me to let go of them and pass them on to someone else who could enjoy them. I knew it was okay for me to hold onto the memories of all the hours of fun and imagination they gave to me as a kid. I could see how they finally led me to hop in the saddle and learn how to ride as an adult. I could observe how important it is to never let go of fulfilling your childhood dreams.

★ ★ ★

A True Friend: My BFF

Dear Jeff,

I write this letter with sadness and regret, but I didn't want this to go unnoted. It has been years since I sat down and wrote you a handwritten letter, and I will say this does bring back memories of when you were in the Marine Corps and we used to write all those letters back and forth to each other. I can even think of that Dear John (or, as I like to call it, Dear Jane) letter you sent via FedEx to me fondly and smile about it today. They weren't kidding about their slogan, "When it positively has to be there overnight."

Anyway this makes me stop and reflect about our twenty-plus-year friendship and all we have been through. If you would have asked me two years ago where I thought our friendship would be in the coming years, I would have told everybody, no matter what, we would always be the best of friends with each other because we worked too hard at gaining the friendship and keeping it up over the years. We have been through way too much with each other (the birth of my son, different loves, new jobs and careers, different cities, laughter, understanding, heartache and grief over the loss of my father, as well as other family health scares plus so much more) to lose the friendship. It saddens me now to say how wrong I was. The past year has just been such a debacle when it comes to where I thought our friendship stood, and I guess we only have each other to blame. I never saw you until today since you moved back from Florida, and I ran into you by accident.

I didn't go to your engagement party. I know I hurt you, and I guess we both have our reasons. I do miss what we had for so many years, and I wanted you to know that above anything else. It happens. I guess people grow out of friendships. I just never thought that was going to be us, but people do change and have to make adjustments according to life.

With that said, I want to wish you the best in everything you do. I hope for nothing but a life filled with complete happiness and love and one that challenges you in positive ways. I will think of you often and pray that God is protecting and blessing you and watching over you. And I hope you find your passions, even if they are ever-changing, and follow them.

God bless you, Jeff, and best wishes on every endeavor that comes upon you. I will think of you fondly and cherish the memories I have, and I do understand why we are where we are. No matter how unfortunate and sad, I really do understand.

With all my love,
Kristin

★ ★ ★

I could write a book in and of itself about Jeff's and my friendship and the course it has taken over twenty-five years. I am filled with so much love from it. Outside of family, I have worked the hardest at this friendship for its continued growth, and I can only hope and pray it will sustain my lifetime. Fortunately this letter prompted Jeff and I to get together to sit and talk about how we were both feeling at this certain point in our lives with our friendship.

Even though it took some time to get back to it, Jeff and I usually talk once a week. We have lost each other at different times in our lives because of relationships we were in with individuals who could not accept our friendship, our bond. In fact I had said to Jeff just a week or so ago that whomever I am with will have to accept our friendship and I don't ever want to have to go through someone's nonacceptance of it just because he doesn't understand it.

Jeff and I tell each other just about almost everything, and sometimes it is too much information, but we end up laughing so hard once we realize we have pushed the envelope with sharing information about each other's lives. So many people have asked over the years why we just don't date and get together, and I think we both know that is not the purpose we are intended to fulfill in each other's life. I think everyone needs that friend of the opposite sex to have in his or her life to talk about the people he or she is dating, to get the honest responses, to throw thoughts and ideas off each other, and so forth. The most important reason in my eyes to have a friend like Jeff is to love him like family.

★ ★ ★

Age Is Not a Factor When It Comes to Being Friends

My dear friend Amber,

There are some people (a few in fact) that you are just comfortable enough to share every aspect of your life with, and you, my dear friend, is thankfully one of those people for me, and for that I am truly grateful to have you as a friend in my life. I love how you love the details of every story and don't ever want anything left out. I love how, when I tell you what I want to do next in my life, like move down to Nashville and write number-one songs for country music, you don't laugh but always say, "If that is something you want to do, I think you should do it," where most others just laugh at me.

You're such a great supporter of your friends, and you really work at staying connected with so many people. Yet at the same time, you understand, when others get so busy, you know how to just pick up where that friendship left off.

I also love that you are the best travel buddy ever. Your carefree, laid-back way about you just makes vacationing so enjoyable. Even when I know I get cranky, you just roll with it. We need to go on another trip together very soon. It has been so wonderful to have you in my life. I am truly blessed.

I also enjoy how you are willing to include everybody on a night out, no matter who they are and how you know them. You have blossomed into such a wonderful young woman, and it's been nice to see you get out of your comfort zone. I love having you in my life. Your free spirit is so refreshing to have around, and I know, when I don't see you for a month, I miss you.

I can't wait to see what life has to offer us and to share the stories with each other along the way. Here's to many more years of friendship.

Love you, girlie,
Kristin

★ ★ ★

I met Amber during one of the biggest transitions in my life, when I decided to follow my passion for cooking. I knew the only way I could do this, since I had zero experience in a professional kitchen, was to go back to school and get my culinary degree. There I was at thirty-six years old in a classroom for the first time again in this funny little outfit that we were required to wear: black-and-white checked pants, a white chef coat, black nonslip shoes, a white Pillsbury Dough Boy puffy hat, and that damned white neckerchief we all had to learn how to tie the proper way.

Amber was an instant friend. We had so many classes together that first semester, and we made sure we had many more with each other over the next two years. We studied together, went to the gym before our seven o'clock class, and worked out together. We were each other's motivation, and it is so great to have that kind of friend in your life. I look at Amber's and my rapport, and this is a prime example of there being no age barriers to true friendship. She is in her midtwenties (yet with an old soul), and I am in my early forties with a young heart. And we are as dear of friends as we were that first year we met. We have traveled the world together and built moments and memories together.

But most importantly we have given each other understanding and support, unconditionally and wholeheartedly. I love that Amber and I have found such an unexpected beautiful friendship that I know, believe, and feel in my heart will last a lifetime.

★ ★ ★

The Magic Kingdom

Dear Marybeth,

It was so good to see you, get caught up on life and family, and share old times from school. I am truly grateful we were able to reconnect. You still have the greatest laugh that is so contagious and makes me laugh just thinking about it. Thank you so much for allowing Christopher and me to have a set of your allocated tickets to the theme parks. This has always been a favorite vacation destination for us over the years. We loved hanging out with you, and yes, by the end of the night, my feet were killing me, and I had a few blisters, but it was all worth it, having had such a great time exploring all the parks.

With any luck we can get together on one of my next visits as well, and I hope all is well with you and your family and you are enjoying your summer. Thank you so much again for offering any help to Christopher while he is living down in the Orlando area. That was very nice of you and very comforting for me. It is crazy how much I miss him. I know he is a young man and all, but it just puts my mind a little at ease knowing someone I know is close by.

Take care, and thank you so much again. It's nice to have old friends.

Thank you for everything,
Kristin

★ ★ ★

I have known Marybeth since grade school, but I probably hadn't seen her since high school graduation. It was fun reliving some stories from way back then and talking about things I hadn't thought of in so many years. I am sure it was a little funny for my son to hear about his mom when she was in grade school and high school. This is by far one of the greatest assets of social media, being able to reconnect with old friends.

★ ★ ★

In today's day and age of the Internet, I do believe that writing a personalized note or letter and sending via e-mail instead of handwriting it and sending it by snail mail can still be very beautiful and heartwarming. I hope you will see that in this series of words written to my old friend from high school.

A Heart Full of Love: Organ Donation Can Save a Life

I came across this poem when going through a box of letters I had saved. I had written it to a friend of mine in high school back when we were about seventeen years old after her ski accident:

When hope and courage fail and only fear is strong,
your heart will sing as in the past, an unforgotten song.
No burden is too heavy, and no sorrow we face is too deep
and devastating in your deepest hour of faith.
The light fills your world, though your skies are not so blue.
Even on the darkest days, the sunshine still peeks through.
In time of trouble, sorrow, and care,
be still and listen; know we are here
to comfort and give you the strength you need.
Whatever the problem, we will be there for you whenever
you want to see.
In the dark hours of the night, you open your eyes, and yet
there is no light.
Upon the ceiling your eyes have glanced, you think of
the day's events, and you go into a trance. Around the
room, all you see are the beautiful flowers from friends
indeed.
You close your eyes, and to a surprise, you see the wonderful
light embroider around Colleen Sweeney.

★ ★ ★

Dear Colleen,

As I sat and reread that poem I wrote you almost twenty-five
years ago, it makes me think of the trials and tribulations in life
we have been faced with since then and the joys and blessings
we have received from those experiences. I feel blessed that I
have been able to follow along on some of your journeys in life
through Facebook, Tommy's Care Page, and the lovely news
stories they have been done about you and your family over
the years. You have showed incredible strength, joy, love, and

sensitivity for others' feelings. You have allowed us to see your raw emotions through your writings, and you have had such articulation through it all.

I am proud to call you an old friend, and I have admired how you have carried yourself through all of it. Even though our involvement in each other's lives has been through social media (other than our twentieth high school reunion), I still think of you as a dear friend in my life of fond memories, which I am truly grateful for. I reflect on you and your family often, and I am always keeping you in my thoughts and giving prayers to those in your life who need them.

Thank you for being you. You are an absolute inspiration.

From an old friend with love,
Kristin

★ ★ ★

Colleen and I have been writing back and forth for the past several years, and I absolutely love it. She is an amazing writer in her own right, and I can only hope one day that she will write a memoir of her family's journey. I know it would be one of the most beautiful reads put together.

In 2008, when Colleen and I met up at our twentieth high school reunion for the first time, we sat face-to-face, and I could see in her eyes what she and her husband were going through. Colleen's story, from what I can say, is one of the most incredible stories of faith and miracles that I love. Our lives sometimes become incredible journeys that, even when we look back, we don't know how we got through other than by the grace of God. Our friends can play so many different roles at various times on our journey, and I know I am blessed to have a friend like Colleen on my life's journey.

★ ★ ★

Funny Guy: More Importantly a Friend..... Throw Glitter

Dear Chris,

It is only appropriate that I end this year with a letter to you, seeing as I started these twelve months asking for a big favor from you. I wanted to know if you could help my son when he moved to LA, even if it were only to give him some advice on how to deal with the crazy things that happened out there. Without fail or hesitation, you said of course. You said you would always help out those from your hometown, and you said you would help him because I was always nice to you in high school.

I can't express how much this meant to me besides saying it filled my heart with gratitude. Once a parent has to let go of her only child into adulthood as he moves across country, just knowing there was someone out there I knew, who was willing to help him, gave me the peace of mind I needed, so thank you for that.

The month of December always becomes one of reflection for me, and I wanted to take a minute to reflect on what I consider to be wonderful moments that I shared with you this year. However minimal you might think they may be, they were impactful and what I needed at the right time.

First, it was great to see you perform in LA at the Laugh Factory, and it wasn't lost on me that I was able to experience you in your true element, watching you follow your dreams and passions. To have my son be a small part of your journey this year is something he will surely and always remember as the years go by and he reflects one day on his first year in LA. Who would have ever thought when we were in high school that my son would someday be shooting your YouTube videos. It's pretty cool if you ask me.

As I sit and scroll through our Facebook messages from this year, I wanted to let you know that I will always cherish these short and simple conversations. On my end for some reason, they were wholehearted conversations, and I don't always feel I can do that with everyone, but I did sense I could do that with you and show my vulnerability. This was probably because you show yours each and every day to your friends and fans through all you post on Facebook and other social networks and especially when you get up on stage to perform. Most of the time, you were a man of few words, but it was just the words I needed to hear. A simple "thank you" goes a long way with me.

It wasn't until August that our paths would physically cross again, specifically at your show in Royal Oak, and your one simple question to me, "Is he the one?" was the reality check I needed to hear, even though I already knew in my heart that the answer was no. It is what I needed, someone to say to me to help me realize what I wasn't doing for myself and to help me get back on the path I had set out on earlier in the year, to create this incredible life of opportunity for myself. I needed to continue to follow my dreams and passions, so I really need to thank you because, for whatever reason you asked me that question, I am so glad you did, even if it were a reality I didn't want to hear.

I share all of this with you because it is the impact that your kindness has had on me. Your genuine curiosity, concern, and willingness to share the books that worked for you were exactly what I needed to keep me lifted up. I think I will remember most the phone call we shared this year. When I sent you the message explaining what I was trying to do in reviving the lost art of a personalized written letter, you instantly asked me for my number, picked up the phone, and gave me some of the most encouraging words, that is, I can have anything I set my mind to if I just believe in myself.

Chris, that is more than some of my closest friends and family members have done for me this year when I explained to them what I wanted to do, and I do feel truly blessed that you called me that day. And whether you wanted it or not, you became a part of my journey into this wonderful world of writing and sharing my expressions one day for many to see.

I know I have said this before, but just know I can't say it enough. You are an inspiration. Look at all you have accomplished not just this year but in your life. To watch you continue to follow your dreams and passions and to see you sharing how the struggles have been some of the most pivotal points of sheer determination for you, I am sure it has prompted more than just me to continue on the road of following one's dreams. So not just for me but for all of those who have wanted to reach out to you and haven't, I wanted to say thank you for being you. Thank you for the positive impact you have had on my life. You are loved.

Cheers to an even more incredible 2014, my friend,
Kristin

★ ★ ★

Over the past several years, I have loved watching my high school friend Chris go after his dreams by following his passions and achieving them one after the other. He has shared so many little inspirational messages of understanding that I have greatly appreciated.

How many times have we wanted to say something special to someone but just never did? I say, "Live with no regrets." I am also glad that I can still text Chris today and say one of the favorite things I love to say to him when he crosses my mind: Love Your Face!! And I get the same message in return.

★ ★ ★

To All the Amazing Women I Met in 2013

Karen, Jen, Lori, Mary, Estee, Tricia, Kacee, Jessica, Logan, Hailey, Wendy, Kristin, Monique, Becky, Lauren, Alexa, and Misty,

As I reflect on the year for a moment, the first thing that comes to mind are all the strong women I have met this year: the independent women, the thoughtful thinkers, the ones who have supported me on my journey wholeheartedly and unconditionally, those I can tell anything to, and the ones who would never think of judging me for decisions I have made but have reminded me to own them. I think of the women I have shared a glass of wine and incredible conversations with, the women who challenge me to be the best person I can be, and those who encourage me to continue on this journey of following my dreams and passions, and I feel truly blessed.

When I started this year, I never thought for a second that I would have met any one of you, but as my year unfolded and I learned how to soften my heart, forgive myself and others, and live my life filled with joy, love, peace, and gratitude, one by one, you unfolded into my life, and for each and every one of you, for all the uniqueness you have brought into my life, I am truly grateful. I just wanted to take a moment to say thank you from the bottom of my heart for being a part of my life now, for I am blessed because of it.

Thank you for sharing in my 2013. It will be a year I will never forget, and here is to an even more incredible journey in 2014.

From my heart to yours,
Kristin

★ ★ ★

Bourbon Buddy: You Expanded Not Only My Palate but My Life Too

Dear Andrew,

As I sit here in a coffee shop in Bellevue, I realize you are probably on your way right now, moving to North Carolina. I don't know if it has actually hit me yet that you're gone, but I am sure it will once I get back to work next week. I am not too sure how I am going to feel about all the changes, but I promise you I will keep an open mind and be kind in the process.

I am very reflective as I sit here and think of all the things we have been through in the past sixteen months. Every little story I will reminisce about here had an impact on me and comes from a place in my heart. I remember the first time I had to come to you and talk with you about everything that was happening. Your initial response was to ask me if I were just being too sensitive. I stared at you for what seemed to be an eternity, for this was my first insight into your management style. And then I finally said I would have to get back to you on that question. I don't remember how much time went by before I came back with my response, but I can recollect the look on your face and the tonality in your voice after I looked at you and said, "Sensitivity is often misconstrued for intuitiveness." And you said, "Okay, let's sit and talk."

In that moment, we built an incredible trust with each other, and now that you are gone, I so recognize the importance that it was for both of us and the significance of trust for any relationship. I also realize we made a choice every day to work together as a team and to support and help each other. Within the trust we built for each other, we knew we would never allow the ship to sink, and I can't thank you enough for all of it and for believing in me. I don't think either one of us knew the journey we had ahead of us, and it was a hell of a route for me, probably because it wasn't a planned one but something I fell back into. And especially now, I am truly grateful to have shared it with you.

One thing I will remember with an incredible fondness in my heart is the laughter, and you have one hell of a laugh, my friend. It makes me chuckle as I sit here and think about it, along with all the inappropriate things we would laugh about, and it puts warmth in my heart and a smile on my face.

If you can't tell by now, I am writing this letter to thank you not only for your constant support but mostly for the confidence you showed in me. You knew when to push me and lift me up. You knew how to make me think, and you taught me so much. Not only did you teach me about food, flavors, bourbon, and bitters, but you taught me more about myself as a chef, and you restored in me why I went to culinary school in the first place.

I will remember many mornings picking you up way before sunrise. I will remember your responses to my incessant questions and all the inappropriate conversations that would make Tyler squirm. And you definitely knew how to do that and take things to a whole new level. There is so much more that you bestowed upon me that I will take with me for a long time to come, specifically how much of yourself you shared not only with me but with everyone else.

I also want to acknowledge that you are the kind of person who could really bring a team together by your actions alone, and then you would pose a question to the team to have everyone interact with each other. My favorite one to this day was, "What is your favorite breakfast?" It wasn't the question, but as always, your response to your own questions was so cathartic, and the interaction would just set such a great tone and mood in the kitchen. You knew how to engage the staff and communicate, and because of this, you were respected.

There is one thing I feel I never gave enough justice to thanking you for, to tell you what it really meant to me, and that is because of the level of emotion it still brings to me to this day. I don't know that I can articulate even now what it meant to me when you gave me one of your father's Hungarian cookbook. This was probably one of the most beautiful gestures anyone has ever shown me, let alone a boss. I knew what your relationship with your father meant to you, and I won't ever forget the look in your eyes on the day you so tragically lost him. I will always remember a few months later when you called me in the office and said you had something for me. You started telling me you had been going through your books at home, and you had come across this particular cookbook of your father's. And you sat and reminisced a little about your father and his Hungarian heritage, and then you said how proud you were of me and how far I had come. And you said you felt I would really enjoy this cookbook and the history it had in it, and you wanted me to have it. When I think of that moment and the sentiment behind it, it never fails to bring a tear to my eye and love to my heart.

Too many times in life, we pay tribute to the people we love—those who have inspired us, played pivotal roles in our lives, and helped us on our journey to become a better person—when they are gone. This letter is my way of paying tribute to you now, to say thank you and to let you know how grateful I am that we met and formed a friendship. I want to say thanks for all the memories you have given me and everything you taught me.

From the bottom of my heart, I will cherish it all. I also want to say how happy and excited I am for you right now on this huge step you have taken on this next part in your life's journey. I can't wait to see what it will bring you. Until we meet again.

From my heart and hand to yours,
Kristin

Southern Gentleman: Chef, Self-Taught Farmer, Boss, and Mentor Extraordinaire

Dear Tyler,

I sit here with such mixed emotions of complete happiness for you and utter sadness that you are no longer going to be a part of my life at work. My eyes actually well up with tears when I think about it. Honestly I am still in shock that you're leaving, but wow! What an amazing, incredible career you've had so far, and I can't wait to hear more about what is ahead and watch Southall's progress. Thirteen years in one place is almost unheard of for a chef or anyone at that point these days. Oh, how I wish I could have seen you in those early days of you being on the line, cooking your ass off with Sean Brock. When asked about you from others since you left, I have said the best way to describe your career is that you took Sean's legacy, kept its integrity alive, and created your own amazing legacy not only in the kitchen but also with the creations of the vegetable garden at Glen Leven and the Double-H cattle farm.

To be able to be a part of this with you for eighteen months will be a highlight for me in my career, and I feel very blessed to have worked a few of your specialty dinners with visiting chefs during my time with you. How about those twice-poached eggs we accidently did for Ashley Christensen? She was such a good sport about the situation, and it was actually very incredible for me to see the things such talented, award-winning chefs could do in pressure situations as food is going out and you are short two dishes. What I enjoyed the most about that dinner in particular was seeing the respect and friendship you have with Ashley. It was so heartfelt and admirable the amount of respect that was shared between the two of you.

Okay, let me get back on track here, but I am chuckling a little because this letter is typical of most of our conversations, all over the place yet heartfelt. When I first started my job, I had no idea about anything I was walking into. I had no idea who you were. I didn't know much about Southern cuisine. I had never worked in a restaurant kitchen before, but I was open to learn about it all. You know me, I did my research and approached my job with an open mind. I wanted to, and I think I did show a strong work ethic and organizational skills, along with the ability to cook great food for large groups of people.

Change came quickly for me, and I will always remember one of our first conversations in the cooler with the situation at hand. You approached me and said Andrew had come to you and informed you of his and my conversation. You said you understood, and then you asked me to be patient. I looked at you with my left eyebrow raised, shaking my head up and down and saying okay. In that moment we built our trust with each other. You never let that trust down with me, and I will always remember and cherish this. You have one of the strongest characters I have ever come across in my career as a chef, and that is hard to come by in this industry with everyone's egos getting in the way.

You know I was thinking the other day about how things used to be in the kitchen with the old crew, and I realize now how I could have appreciated it more on a day-to-day basis. I miss the laughter, even all the inappropriate cringeworthy conversations that brought on a lot of the laughter. I miss those things the most, but also I pine for the friendships, the genuine caring that was shared among us. I miss those irritating moments because, in those times, we made strong bonds and built friendships. Without question, one of the things I yearn for the most, Tyler, are our conversations, so thought-provoking and full of analogies that I would have to ask you what they meant half the time.

Oh God, I really did learn a lot from you, not just about the industry or how to properly slice a potato on a mandolin so you could get full coverage in the pan. (That still makes me laugh.) But I learned a lot about life from you. The experiences you were willing to share helped me deal with the experiences my son has been going through. You have helped me deal with an aging mother with Alzheimer's, just by your compassion for my circumstance alone. All of your kind words always came right when I needed them the most. And the empathy you consistently showed me as I was on my unexpected medical leave this summer speaks leaps and bounds of the type of person you truly are. You are such an old soul with so much to share, and I thank you, my friend, for sharing so much of it with me. I am eternally grateful and extremely blessed to have found you, especially in this time of my life.

I also want to thank you for how much you have been there for me since you have left and to thank you for all the great pieces of advice you have given me. I do feel blessed for all I have learned from you, and I know it will help me in my future endeavors. I essentially want to say thank you for everything and to acknowledge how you have inspired me in so many ways. So thank you, thank you, thank you for being so wonderful and acting as a willing participant in my life's journey. I am truly grateful for all of it. Until we meet again, my friend.

From my heart and hand to yours,
Chin chin,
Kristin

My Hyster Sister

Dear Sarah,

This letter is very overdue but still just as important nonetheless if it had been written four months ago. I wanted to let you know how much your messages to me the day before my surgery meant to me. I was in such a place of feeling alone and not quite understanding what I was about to go through, but I was doing my best to figure it out and prepare myself for the weeks ahead. I think you and I both know how blessed we are to have a friend like Jeff in our lives. I know he went out of his way to contact you, knowing you had been through this the previous year and knowing I was here in Nashville without family and just a few friends. He wanted to give me the best support he knew how to, and that was you.

When your first message came through, I have to admit I was a bit confused, and then as soon as I realized it was from you and Jeff had contacted you to see if you would reach out to me, a beautiful calm and warmth came over me that helped me so much, not only at that moment but in the coming weeks. I don't think I could do the feeling justice through these words here. In the matter of minutes that it took you to send me those messages, I no longer felt alone through this. I held onto your words and all of your advice in the following weeks, and in my darkest moments of pain and uncertainty, the words you wrote got me through.

So from the bottom of my heart, thank you, thank you, thank you! I am so grateful that you were there for me, especially since you were lying in your own hospital bed recovering from your tonsillectomy. What you were able to give me with your beautiful, heartfelt words will stay with me for years to come. You helped me let go of the fear and allowed me to open up my heart and feel all the blessings everyone was giving me instead of sitting in a bed of worry.

Sarah, I really do believe that how you were able to make me feel before my surgery helped me leaps and bounds in my recovery process. My heart is full, and my blessings are bountiful. Thank you, my old friend, for playing such a pivotal part in my healing process and road to recovery. From my heart and hand to yours, I love you.

Kristin

Chapter 3
Unexpected Inspiration from Complete Strangers

Sometimes This Can Be the Best Kind of Inspiration

Sometimes we never know when inspiration will hit us. It can either graze us softly or take our breath away when we feel it. It can come from funny banter between two morning talk show hosts, a couple's love story, a book, song lyrics, or notes from someone who enlisted in the Marines just days after September 11 to serve our country and is now pursuing his dreams and giving back. It can be from a trio who are preserving American history or just watching a girl follow her passions with the support of her family, having then made her dreams come true.

Who has inspired you in your life? The following letters are to complete strangers, people I have never met whose stories I have fallen in love with and have inspired me on my life's journey.

A Dynamic Duo: And They Do It Live

Dear Regis and Kelly,

I just needed to take a minute out of my day to thank the both of you for the joy you give me every morning that I get a chance to watch you. Your show, especially the first twenty minutes, is so funny. To be able to start my day with laughter is wonderful, and I am truly grateful for that. There is absolutely no show out there like yours. It's timeless, and you have perfected it. More importantly the dynamics between the two of you is so heartfelt, and the genuine love you feel from the whole set (all the people such as Michael Gelman and Art Moore) around you comes through into my room every morning and helps jump-start my day in such a positive way.

Thank you again for all you do to bring happiness, joy, and love into my life, and I am sure for many others that it is truly appreciated. And I am absolutely grateful for it.

Sincerely,
Kristin Horvath

★ ★ ★

When I reread this letter, I have to say it absolutely 100 percent applies to Kelly and Michael. I love watching them when I get the chance. You never know what they are going to say or where the conversation is going to go in a fun, humorous way of course, and if I think back, it would have applied in the days of Regis and Kathy Lee too.

Now that I think about it, I probably watch this show more than any other out there over so many years. Wow, that makes my heart fill up with even more love and gratitude when I think of the years of laughter I have shared with all of the different cohosts. It's a job well done.

During this time in my life when I wrote this letter, I was relearning the practice of gratitude. My parents did instill it in me as a child through our daily prayers to give thanks, but somewhere along the way, I had lost it, and I knew I wanted it back in my life. A way for me to do this was through writing these letters. Writing to me can be so healing and almost spiritual, and it's a great way to share thoughts of gratitude and thanks to others, especially those who aren't expecting it. I can attest for me personally that my life is so much better not only when I think of the things I am grateful for first thing in the morning but when I write them out. There is just something in it that works for me to put these thoughts to pen and paper.

Representing the "D"

Dear Marshall,

This note comes to you with thoughts of gratitude and thanks (in more ways that I can take the time to sit here and explain) on behalf of my whole family. Your name has come up in the house more so than not in the last six months, and it finally clicked with me that I needed to sit down and write you this letter, especially after my seventy-five-year-old mother got a wee bit choked up when talking to me about your most recent Chrysler commercial. Conversations of your commercial consumed my mother's Super Bowl Monday in a good way. She went to your defense when friends questioned why you were chosen to do that commercial, especially with all "your problems." And she told me that she said, "Why wouldn't they choose him, for he has faced his demons with great avail and stood by and supported this city when most others have just simply walked away and left it to fail?" My mother said she felt you get it probably better than anyone else and you have come a long way. I was so proud of how she spoke of you, and for that moment, she didn't stand in judgment of you, but she stood up for you.

Your ad for the Chrysler 200 passes with flying colors here in our Chrysler born and bred home, and I just wanted to thank you for being a part of the restoration of a company that knows how to make a comeback, and it's good to see you being utilized in a way that can have such a positive impact. I hope all is well in your life, and just know that this note does come with the most intimate feelings of thanks and gratitude for everything you have shared with us and all you do to help this city stand up. You are inspiring a younger generation to want to do the same instead of fearing the unknown and walking away. As my mother would say, "Stay strong and be true to yourself."

With gratitude and thanks,
Kristin Horvath

★ ★ ★

At times I am so inspired that I have to immediately sit down to get out my thoughts and write them down so I don't lose that initial inspiration and can then collect my thoughts in their truest, purest forms. Then other times I find myself feeling a little silly about the person I want to write to so I can say thanks for the inspiration. So sometimes I wait to see if those feelings are true or if they will subside. I listen to my intuition mostly and my heart.

With this particular individual, I had written another letter before this one, but because I probably felt silly about writing it, I never followed through with sending it. I want to share it here today because, as I reread these letters, years after they were originally written, I am taken right back to that time in my life and everything that was going on when I wrote them.

When Eminem's *Recovery* CD came out, my son and I could bond over it because we were both such huge fans. My son and I have gone on some long road trips together, and sometimes the music we listen to doesn't always resonate with each other or just the mood at the moment of being confined in a car for hours at a time. But at any time, we always agree on Eminem. We don't just listen to his music. We talk about his lyrics because I firmly believe he is a lyrical genius and what he really meant by what he said. My son and I have truly spent many hours bonding with Eminem playing in the background. When a parent can bond with a child over a musical artist, at least for me, I am truly grateful for those moments, and that is why I wanted to share these specific letters. More importantly, that is why I wanted to write them to capture those moments that built the memories between a mother and son.

Recovery

Dear Marshall,

I write this letter with thoughts of thankfulness and gratitude. Have you ever had a thought that continuously reappears in your mind's eye, to the point where you realize you needed to stop, sit, and get it jotted down on paper? Well, this letter is just that, a thought in my head that keeps popping up, so I figured it was best to sit and put it down with my pen and paper, and maybe my thoughts could start generating something greater.

I essentially wanted to take this opportunity to say, "Thank you." You see, your most recent music and the life's battles you have shared with your fans within your music resonates with my son and me. For him to see this "recovery" you have gone through helps make his world seem less shattered than I know he has been seeing it as, and I am truly grateful for that. It's not so much your addictions and demons that he can relate to, but it's your persistence to get through these life-altering changes. More specifically, I think it's the loss and grief he sees you dealing with, and he gets that. Unfortunately he has had that, and I think he is trying to get past it and through it. Actually I think he is trying to commemorate that loss he has had the way you have memorialized the loss of your dear friend in your life.

I am grateful he has something in your music that helps him with the thoughts going through his head. As close as we are, there are just things kids have a hard time talking to parents about. I am sure you know, as a parent, it's the things that happen within your child's life that really matter the most.

My son and I bond over your music, and I love that we can have many a conversation about it, what he thinks you are trying to say and mean by the words you choose. I take interest in the things he takes an involvement in, and you happen to be someone he is passionate about from an artistic impression—the words you write, the meaning you give to your life with the analogies and realities you choose, and the ways you share all of it. Not only do you put it out there, but the analogies and correlations to your realities have so many dimensions to it, and it is so powerful.

So I want to thank you for having the ability and strength to share your life experiences, and just know that others find inspiration in it.

With thoughts of gratitude,
Kristin Horwath

★ ★ ★

My son is reading most of these letters for the first time, just like the rest of you, and I am sitting here kind of laughing, just wondering what is going through his head. What do you think of your mom's writings so far, Christopher? For years when my son and I would talk, we would always ask, "How are you?" and "What are you doing?" When I would tell him I just wrote another letter, I could tell he didn't always get it.

I will never forget the day he finally got what I was doing. Of course it was a movie that helped him understand my passion for writing letters. He had just seen the movie *Her*, and he called me right away and said, "I finally get it, Mom. I finally get why you love writing the letters you do." And he explained to me how Joaquin Phoenix's character worked for a company that wrote letters to people and how his character had a book published of the best letters he had written for them. I will never forget that moment and saying to my son, "Remember to always follow your heart and be thankful for everything along the way."

As an introduction to my next letter, I would like to say this. I grew up in a very patriotic family even though none of my immediate family members ever served in the armed forces. We grew up understanding what it was to live in America and to have our freedoms, and we understood the price people paid so we could have all we had. We flew our American flag in front of the house. We celebrate on the Fourth of July and understood why. We acknowledged Memorial Day. We visited our nation's capital, and we prayed on a daily basis that all troops were being watched over, protected, and blessed by God's graces wherever they were.

This is probably why I feel so compelled to give back to those who give me my freedom every day and why I find inspiration from those who have served. It's because of the compassion that was instilled in me throughout my life for those who put their lives on the line.

Thank You for Your Service

Dear Stephen,

With sincerest gratitude and thanks, I write this letter to you. This is a bit of a story as to how I got to this point, but if you could just bear with me a moment, I promise it's a nice one. I will be honest and say that, until last Sunday, May 15, I didn't even know your name. And then a coworker said to me, "Hey, my cousin is playing at the Hoedown today." I asked, "Who is your cousin?" And we hopped on the computer and Googled you so she could just show me who you were. My first comment was "Great T-shirt!" (It said, "Save a Horse; Ride a Cowboy.") We chuckled. I said some other things on a quick observation. She said she was your cousin through her husband connected to your mother. (I think they are first cousins.)

I was looking at your website as Lori went into this story about what you had done with your life, and the story she was telling me made me stop clicking on the mouse and listen.

I listened to her tell me of your time spent in the service as a Marine, fighting over in both Iraq and Afghanistan. She told me about how you were injured and told you would never walk again. She said that, now by the grace of God, an experimental surgery, and sheer determination, you were walking and pursuing your career in country music.

The only words that could come out of my mouth at that moment were "Wow!" That's an absolutely amazing and incredible story of heroism. I couldn't even begin to imagine what going through any of it was like. So we went about our day at work, and at one point when I came back to my little kitchen office, your Google info was still up on my computer screen. And when I sat down, I knew I wanted to know more. Out of curiosity and intrigue, I started clicking and reading away, and I was truly amazed still by what Lori had told me, but then more so to hear it in your own words through your music and interviews and seeing the pictures from your time in the service to the present day, all you have posted on social media.

It made me really stop and reflect, and I was drawn in more. This time I was suddenly feeling a great amount of admiration for how you were sharing your story and what you are doing with your talents to support, raise money, and bring attention to our veterans who, like you, served our country and left their blood, sweat, and tears in the fields of war so we as Americans could have our freedom. So for all you do for those who can't, I want to say thank you.

Two days after I talked to Lori, I realized your other cousin, her stepdaughter Britney, also works with me in a different kitchen. So when I saw her, I stopped dead in my tracks and said, "Hey, I hear your cousin was in town playing at the Hoedown." Brit got a big smile on her face, and you could tell she was emoting such a sense of pride. I looked at her and said, "I know. Lori told me his story." She said, "No, let me tell you. Even though I am much younger than he is, I always knew he was going to do something amazing with his life." When she heard you were going into the Marines, right then and there, she knew you would be a hero. She said the more amazing thing about you is that not only are you the hero she knew you would be, but you continue to be a hero with all the shows you put on to raise money for veterans and their families. You can tell how much your family in Michigan loves you and how proud they are to say they know you and call you family, which I am sure you see and feel from them every time you are in town.

All in all, I wanted to thank you for the service you gave our country, everything you do for our veterans so they don't feel alone, and the inspiration you have unexpectedly provided me. I am truly honestly grateful to know your story.

Sincerely,

Kristin A. Horvath

★ ★ ★

I wrote Stephen another letter a few months after I had sent him the first one, and this is part of that letter. As an artist and creative person yourself, Stephen, I hope you understand when you feel inspired you have to capitalize on that moment. Carpe diem. Seize the day or really the inspiration in this case. And I also hope you understand that you don't always know where your inspiration is going to come from, but once it hits, you need to write it down.

Essentially I am trying to say that I didn't ask for it. I didn't know it was going to happen, but your story has inspired me

tremendously. I am writing to you yet again because you were
the inspiration behind these words:

> Life came upon me one day
> And told me a story I didn't know.
> True inspiration were the words I heard,
> And I almost let them go.
> A life someone else lived
> That I don't even know,
> He was just a simple country kid
> Whose heart told him where to go.
> He came back a man, broken and bruised.
> Told he'd never walk again.
> He figured what this life gave him
> Was for no one else to choose.
> An undeniable born hero,
> He knew he had nothing left to lose.
> Kentucky born and bred
> With Michigan summers
> And thoughts of his granny up north
> Always in his heart and his head,
> A country music man in his dreams
> With sounds of Motown running upstream
> In the darkest of nights
> With the whiskey in his hand,
> He raises the shot glass up
> And for a single moment
> Remembers when he couldn't stand,
> Being thankful along the way.
> His world would completely change.
> He wears his heart on his sleeve,
> Where you can see right there in ink

How he almost gave his life to God and country.
It is what he has done on our land
To make this a hero's story,
The men and women he continues to fight for
So they don't have to come home alone and worry
About the life they will now live,
Having protected Ol' Glory.

After hearing Stephen's inspirational story, I find myself now having longer conversations with veterans I meet and thanking them for their service and all they did. Stephen's story makes you want to bring awareness to our veterans who have struggles, especially those who suffer from PTSD, so they know they are not alone. This type of story needs to be told more.

Stephen enlisted into the Marines just days after the September 11 attacks. He publicly shares his personal battles while supporting businesses owned and operated by veterans. I think people often don't share their stories because they feel like they are the only ones who are going through it and they feel alone, so once you come across someone who unabashedly puts his or her life story out there, knowing how much it is going to help others and pushes forward to pursue his or her dreams, all the while giving back, says so much about his or her character. That is a truly amazing person in my eyes. Life isn't always about you. It's about how many people you help, inspire, and touch along the way.

When you write letters to complete strangers, you don't know if they actually receive them or not. I don't write these letters to receive responses, but once you do receive a response, no matter how much time has passed, it is always nice.

A few years after these letters were written and as I was putting this story together, I unexpectedly had the opportunity to share my letters again with Stephen through one of his very dear friends, and I received such heartfelt responses from both of them. It was such a feel-good moment felt among all of us, and to be able to give and get such incredible inspiration from complete strangers has definitely been by divine guidance.

During this time of being able to share these letters, Stephen had a personal tragedy and lost his best friend to PTSD. Many prayers were shared during the initial week of Stephen losing Matt, and it was as if spirit came through me to write the following words once I had found out about his loss.

Forever Good-bye:
It's okay. Tomorrow is almost here.
We will be able to raise our glass and share all the stories
we know.
We will be able to smile at each other even though there
will be tears behind our eyes.
We will be able to laugh and say our good-byes.
We will feel you with us as we walk away
And take a part of you in our heart along the way.
We will hear you talking to us, and in those moments, we
will look up into the sky
And be able to say hello instead of this forever good-bye.
Because I am Here:
I am here with you today
In everything that you see.
You don't have to peer around the corner to try to find me.
I am present now in every part of your life.
You don't have to look over your shoulder for me to give
you advice.
I know I am in your thoughts.
But more importantly, I am in your heart

Because I am here with you today
In every possible way.
I am in your breath, and I know you can feel me in your
bones.
I am not just in your darkness,
But I am in your light.
I am in your will that is never going to give up this fight.
Take my hand, and listen to what I have to say
Because I am here with you in every possible way.
I know you're sad and torn, and it is my body today that
you will mourn,
But it is my spirit now that remains with you,
To honor my life like only you can do.

Written in memory of Matthew Allen Harder,
March 21, 1980–February 16, 2014

I have been following Stephen on social media for a few years, and his work still continues to inspired me. The following is another example of how. Stephen, I am responding to your post from Sunday when you were trying to write a new song about coal country and you were looking for ideas. I had some time today, and I came up with this after reading through your posts. I hope you enjoy.

Coal Town

I may have left many years ago
from this little mining town in Eastern Kentucky.
It's a place where I consider home,
even more so
when I went to fight for our country.

It's a place where many of my family members laid down
  their roots,
always remembering them as I was cleaning my rifle
and strapping up my Marine boots.
One day I may move back.
One day I may settle down,
All were the thoughts that would come to my head
as I went to sleep on this cot I called my bed.
As I put on my pack, I longed for those days,
where all I could think of was our Eastern Kentucky coal
  mining ways.
Coal is who we are,
what hasn't been shut down.
I have come too far in life
not to believe in this Eastern Kentucky coal mining town.
I love the air.
It truly grounds me.
I cherish the time with my family.
There is so much love in this Eastern Kentucky coal mining
  town
that surrounds me.
When the coal jobs go,
so does everything else.
It's the trickle-down effect.
My hometown is dying.
All we need is a little help,
and we will be able to stay forever
in a place where neighbors
still offer you fresh garden goods
in this little Eastern Kentucky town
where coal is their livelihood.

★ ★ ★

The following is a letter to an amazing artist whose documentary about her path on the way to country music superstardom was really well done and insightful as to what the whole family went through for her to pursue her passions.

Fearless Inspiration

Dear Taylor,

This letter comes to you with thoughts of gratitude and thanks. Recently on the only day off I had this week, I turned on my Netflix streaming service and started watching your *Fearless* documentary. After watching all three episodes in one fell swoop, I felt that the least I could do was take the time to sit and write this letter to say what an inspiration you and your family truly are. I love seeing people who are following their passions in life, the things they love to do. And seeing the support of one's family in the process is so heartfelt. Observing this quality in others always inspires me to continue to follow the things I am passionate about. How you have taken your life experiences and put them into words and music to share with the world are absolutely amazing. The experiences you share are so honest and genuine. What you have written and sing about resonates with millions, and just knowing one is not alone in his or her own discovery of life can be a coping mechanism to help him or her get through his or her own personal trials and tribulations. You are an inspiration to not only young girls but so many women of all ages.

As I was watching your documentary, I also loved how important it was for you to give thanks to all those fans who have supported you in following your dreams. You can see how authentic your gratitude is toward them. You have taken life so gracefully in stride with all you have gone through, and it is why you are where it has led you today. You are a wonderful role model.

Quite a few years back, my son and I were driving along, and one of your songs came on the radio. (He is going to be mortified that I am sharing this story, but it is a parent's obligation to embarrass his or her kids.) My son turned up the volume, looked at me, and said, "You're listening to my future wife." I chuckled and said, "Yeah, she's pretty great."

For whatever reason, that was just one of those moments between mother and son that have always stuck with me, probably because that was the first conversation we had about my son having a crush on a girl.

Finally I wanted to recognize the family foundation that is so present in your life. It is such a strong testament as to who you are as a young woman, and it is so nice to see how involved your family is in helping you follow your passions and how engaged they are in giving back to your fans. A strong family foundation is just a refreshing thing to see these days.

I had no idea when I pressed play that day that I would find such inspiration in your story, and I just wanted to thank you for that. It helped remind me to stay focused on my dreams and passions because, no matter at what age, they can come true.

I wish you nothing but great blessings in life. I hope so many others can also find inspiration through you and your family as I have.

Sincerely from a future country song writer,
Kristin Horvath

★ ★ ★

As I reread these letters, I am reminded of a conversation my son and I were having many years ago when we would sit and talk about our creative pursuits and what we wanted to do. And I would sit and tell him how I just wanted to be a writer. I could remember seeing the wheels in his head working, and he looked at me and said, "Then every day, Mom, no matter what else is going on, even if it is just for a few minutes, if you want to be a writer, you have to just sit and write, and it will all come together."

During moments like that, I love to reminisce about them in my mind with my son. I love how he processes the ability to get to the things in our life that we are passionate about doing and how we can make it happen for ourselves if we just take even a little step toward it every day and believe.

Sometimes we just need to see it in black and white to know that the feelings in our heart really do have us on the right path. The next two letters are to authors of books I read that had wonderful impacts in my life at the time of reading them. I could write so many letters to so many authors for all the great works I have read.

My Passion Test

Dear Janet and Chris,

To start this note, I want to say thank you for writing and sharing your book, *The Passion Test*. To say it has had such an incredible impact in my life is just the tip of the iceberg. I can say with such excitement that I finally get "it," and I am only on chapter 6.

Six years ago, after my father's unexpected death, I had a profound moment of realizing how important it was to follow your passions in life. So I walked away from my human resources career and went to culinary school. At the time I was passionate about cooking and the feeling it gave me, and I realize now that I was just skimming the surface of what my true passions are.

In the past year, I have read the books *The Secret* and *The Power* by Rhonda Burns, which were a great start for me to learn how to be more open to finding what I truly want out of my life, but I was struggling on how to get those things until now. Because of your book, I have become more open, and I now understand I don't need to worry about the how. But by utilizing the passion test, I am a completely transformed person. I have written out my list of passions, which came to me so easily, and more continue to come to me, which I write down so I don't lose them. (I guess, if they are true passions of mine, I won't lose them.) I have placed several index cards of my top five passions strategically in different places to have easy access to visually seeing them so I always have that constant reminder. I have written my markers for my top five passions, and I am currently working on my vision boards.

I couldn't even wait until I finished your book to write this note to say thank you. I feel truly blessed, and I am completely grateful this book found its way into my life. My cousin was moving across the country from New Jersey to Colorado, and she was stopping home on the way to see her family. I went to see her for an evening and get caught up because it would be several months before I would possibly get to see her again.

After a lovely evening out, we came back to her parents' house and crashed on the couch in front of the television.

There it was sitting on the coffee table, your book, *The Passion Test*. I glanced over at it several times before I finally picked it up, and within two minutes I was hooked. My cousin and I ended up having such a remarkable evening after that, opening up to each other as to what our passions were, and those moments are truly priceless. I look forward to my continued reading of your book and to see what might come, and I thank you again for writing this book. I have absolutely fallen in love with it.

Sincerely,
Kristin A. Horvath

★ ★ ★

As I sit here and work on this, I know a tragic event in my life pushed me in the direction of following my passions. I can only hope for others that they realize they too can follow their passions and they don't have to have that tragic event happen for them to do it. Specifically with this project, aside from the huge accomplishment it is for me, I also hope I can inspire people to either pull out that pen and paper or even hop on their computer to sit and write that letter to someone in their lives who has inspired them or another person just because they were thinking of them and wanted to let them know.

If you really think about it, writing a letter is a feel-good situation all the way around for the person writing it and the individual receiving it. It can bring more love into everyone's life, so why wouldn't we want to do more of that? I know I do, and that is one reason why I wrote all these letters, to share my love with the people it was meant for.

The Secret's Impact on My Life

Dear Rhonda,

What can I say? Thank you. Thank you. Thank you! I am truly grateful you have come into my life by sharing your experiences via your series of books and especially your most recent one, *The Magic*. I know I will continue to read this book over and over because so much good advice is in it, and I know I will get something different and great out of it each time I read it. This book excites me when I think about all I can get out of it, not only for myself but for others in my life.

And so for all this, I truly want to thank you for sharing your experiences. Without them I don't think I would be where I am today. The stories I could share with you as to the positive changes that have come into my life—not only from the thoughts of gratitude and thanks but because I truly believe in the thoughts I have and the experiences I know are still yet to come—excite me the most.

I subscribe to your daily scrolls from *The Secret* website, and it is amazing how, when a scroll pops up in my e-mail, it seems to appear at the most appropriate time and includes information in it that relates exactly to what I or someone else close to me is going through, almost as a sign of reassurance that I am in the right frame of mind. I am grateful for everything I have learned and the way I look at each day of my life and everything in it. And I have you to thank for the knowledge I have gained and how I embrace it.

Here's to wishing you the best in life, and I look forward to your future work. Thank you, thank you, and thank you.

Kristin Horvath

A Lesson in American Pickers History

Dear Mike, Frank, and Danielle,

I wanted to take a moment out of my day to write you a quick note to say thank you for all you do. I am neither a picker nor a collector, other than what has been handed down to me. I don't even go antiquing. So for the past two weeks, I was a bit confused as to why, when I would sit in front of the television, I would find myself literally addicted to watching your show, *American Pickers*, on the Netflix streaming service.

It finally came to me this morning, and I really wanted to share how truly grateful I am for the good warm feeling I have after every episode. The reason I love watching *American Pickers* is threefold.

1. You are all so funny, and I just sit and chuckle throughout the whole show. I mean, who doesn't feel better after they laugh?
2. The people you meet and the stories you tell are just amazing. Who doesn't want to have a little more knowledge of our American history?
3. Your sense of compassion and kindness is so heartfelt and touching. Who doesn't have a tear in his or her eye and want to give back himself or herself after watching you give back five thousand dollars to help a man restart a nostalgic theme park? Who can't understand the love a father has for his son. Knowing you more than likely wouldn't make any money on a purchase, you did it so this particular father could provide physical therapy in the hopes that his son would walk again. It is just wonderful to see, and it was such a selfless act.

Your sense of giving back to others wherever you are in the country is inspiring, so with all this said, I would like to give one thing to your shop so you can pay it forward to someone who would love to have it in his or her collection. The simplistic story behind this license plate topper is that a boyfriend (who probably purchased in Illinois) gave it to me while I was in college about twenty years ago. During the summer months, I worked for AAA of Michigan, planning and charting out maps and trip tickets for people's summer vacations. He thought I would enjoy it, and I did, but it's now time to give it to someone else who will enjoy it. And who better to give it to so this can be done is the three of you. Not only do I speak for myself; I speak for the many others when I say, "Thank you!" for the laughs, kindness, and caring you portray on your show, *American Pickers*. The best to each and every one of you.

Sincerely,
Kristin Horvath

PS. I know the monetary value of this AAA license plate topper is minimal at best, but hopefully in this case, it's the thought that counts. Safe travels.

★ ★ ★

Just a few days after mailing my letter to Iowa, I received a personalized autograph picture in the mail from the three of them: Mike Wolfe, Frank Fritz, and Danielle Colby-Cushman. It said, "To Kristin: Sweet Picking."

I just love this story. As I reread it, I left out as to why I love these three. It's because you can see such passion in what they do. Who wouldn't want to watch people do what they love to do? If you haven't noticed it by now, you will see it more so in the letters to come. I love stories of people who are following their passions because they inspire me on my journey to continue to follow my passions. And that is another reason why I love these guys!

I Love Their Love

Dear Giuliana and Bill,

For a few years now, I have wanted to sit and write this letter to the both of you, but for whatever reason I just never took the time to do it. Sometimes I think it is just a matter of timing for me to be able to be completely open up and speak from the heart as to why I put off certain letters, and I also believe things just happen in divine order.

Writing letters is what I love to do. It is a passion I have because I know receiving a personalized written letter brings joy to those who receive them and because it is a lost art I want to preserve and revitalize. The purposes of my letters are usually to let the person or people receiving the letter know how much they have inspired me in my life and to thank them for that inspiration. I feel it is very important in everyday life to be thankful and grateful not only for the things you have but for the people who have touched your life for the better.

This letter finds its way to the both of you today for several reasons.

1. It is because I love your love story, and I can't thank you enough for sharing it with all of us to see.
2. It is to thank you for putting your stories out there, for you have touched many people's lives over the years with all the experiences you have been through: from breast cancer to fertility treatments and surrogacy to the birth of your bundle of joy, Duke. How you have shared your stories so openly and honestly for others to see, so they know they are not alone in their life journey, is admirable. I can only imagine how many

lives you have not only touched but saved and helped just by sharing these experiences.

3. This reason is twofold: for Bill and all the humanitarian efforts you and your friends have accomplished in Haiti and for Giuliana and all you do with Fab-U-Wish. It is amazing. To see the joy you bring into these people's lives you have reached out to all over the world is a beautiful thing, and I just really wanted to say thank you for sharing all of it.

You give hope to those who felt they had lost faith. You talk very honestly and openly, knowing, if you touch one person's life, it was all worth it. And you seem to do it all selflessly. I would also like to say your sense of humor and ability to laugh with each other is so refreshing.

So for not only me but all those who have thought about it, I want to express a sense of gratitude from the bottom of my heart for showing us the love you have for family and the love you both spread in everything you do. You truly set a beautiful example that more people need to follow of how we need to treat people, what it is to give back, and how important family is in every aspects of our lives.

As some parting words, I'd like to impose the one piece of advice I give my friends who have young children. No matter how tired you get, how busy things may seem, and how much time you feel you don't have, I say stop and enjoy your kids every moment you can, no matter what is going on in your lives. The everyday time you have with your kids goes by quicker than I could have ever imagined. My son's twenty-four years went by in the blink of an eye. I know this is a great new chapter in my son's life to pursue his passions, and I will say I am so thankful that we have had so many memories to hold close to our heart to get us through the times that we are apart. That's what a big part of life is about anyways, isn't it? Building those special moments and creating those memories of love for us to hold onto with our family.

I share this advice with you because it is real-life emotions, and that is exactly what you both have done with your life. You share, you help others, you love, and you learn, and so for all of it, thank you. And thank you for taking the time out of your day to read this. It is from my heart and hand to yours. I wish you nothing but blessings in your life together in the years to come.

With love,
Kristin Horvath

For the Sender

Dear Alex,

You don't know me; nor have you ever heard my name before today. I am writing you this letter to let you know that finding your website, www.forthesender.com, couldn't have been more perfect timing for me. As I like to say, I believe everything is in divine order, and I believe that is exactly what this was for me. I will do my best here to try to articulate why first finding your video, *This Gift*, a thank you to your friend, Dr. Wayne Dyer, "for his support and friendship" and, second, being led to your website gave me exactly what I needed in the moment to help me let go of my fears and my ego and move forward with something I am so passionate about, writing letters.

It was Monday, August 31, and I was sitting outside, enjoying my morning cup of coffee, taking a moment to breathe and be thankful for the day. I started going through my phone to see what was going on. Then in an instant, my breath was taken away. My heart was sad. My eyes were suddenly misting with tears when I saw the news that Dr. Wayne Dyer had passed away the day before. I closed my eyes, took in a deep breath, and released it. And in that moment, I felt his presence surrounding me with so much love, joy, and peace. I can't tell you how long I sat there, taking it all in, but once I finally moved, I pulled up quotes by Dr. Dyer on my phone until I found the one that was perfect for me to post as a tribute to him on my Facebook page. This is how it read: "Every time I pick up a coin on the street, I view it as a symbol of abundance that God sends into my life and feel gratitude. Thank you God for everything. Never do I ask, why only a penny?"

I personally chose that quote because, every time I have picked up a penny for the past decade, I thank God for sending me the penny from heaven as a sign from my loved ones who passed, letting me know they are with me and I am on the right path for my life purpose. In that moment of grief, as I was searching for something to help heal my heart, I felt that Dr. Dyer himself had his hand in helping me to find what I was searching for. After posting Dr. Dyer's quote, I was still feeling the need to find more of him. I needed to feel inspired, so I just started searching the Internet. I started going on anyone's Facebook page that had done work with Hay House. I was searching Dr. Wayne Dyer tributes to see what people were saying. And in that moment, I couldn't find what I was looking for.

I put down my phone and decided to hold onto my own experiences and thoughts of what Dr. Dyer had given to me on my spiritual journey because I knew in my heart that I wouldn't be where I was today without the wisdom he instilled in me through his DVDs, newsletters, PBS specials, work with Louise Hay, and YouTube videos of his speeches I had watched over the years.

As I was sitting in contemplation, I decided to get up and grab my deck of angel cards by Doreen Virtue, and I asked my angels, "What do I need to know today?" The card that came flying out was the Angel Sonya card: "I bring you a message from your deceased loved one: I am happy at peace, and I love you very much. Please don't worry about me." In that moment, in my mind's-eye, I could see people greeting Wayne in heaven, the joy and love everyone was feeling, and the happiness in everyone's hearts as they saw him and he saw them. My grief was eased, and I knew I was to feel joy instead of sadness for all he gave to us, I could still learn from his work that he left us with, and he would still be there to help me on my spiritual journey.

I then found myself going through the motions of grabbing my laptop, a notebook, pens, and my purse and then driving to a coffee shop, sitting there and starting to write yet again. What I was doing wasn't lost on me. It had been over a year since I had written anything of substance to me. I was very aware of what I was writing was coming from a place of love and how I was creating all these incredible feelings from within, and it felt amazing. I went to bed that night not overthinking all the events of the day but instead lying there in peace. I was, however, still very aware that I had lost someone whom I considered a spiritual guru, and that was the last thought I remember having before I fell into a comfortable sleep.

The next morning, I awoke, and I went onto YouTube and listened to one of Dr. Dyer's meditations. Then throughout the day, I was still searching to read tributes from people whose lives Dr. Dyer had touched. An odd exhaustion had come over me, so I lay down for an afternoon nap and fell into a deep sleep. When I got up, I grabbed my phone again, searching for something. I saw that Sunny Dawn Johnston liked the tribute I posted to Dr. Dyer on my page, and for some reason, it really touched me. I felt it deep within. So I went to Sunny's page, and there it was. Sunny Dawn Johnston had shared Alex Woodard's video, *This Gift*. I knew it instantly. It was the tribute my soul had been searching for, not only for the beauty of it all but also what I found next, your website, www.forthesender.com.

I went to the website right away, and I think I literally said aloud, "Oh my God!" as the chills came over me. I became emotional and excited all at once as I read, "For the sender is an inspiring series of books, albums, and concert events featuring a collection of songs based on true letters and stories." I looked up and said, "Oh, God, what do I do with this?" I started slowly clicking on the links and saw reviews from the people I look up to in my life on my spiritual journey: Deepak Chopra, Dr. Christiane Northrup, Cheryl Richardson, and, of course, Dr. Wayne Dyer. I said to myself, "This is what I do. This is what I love. This is so much like my book, and this is amazing!"

My book has been sitting in my Word documents until about two months ago, when I finally put down my ego, set aside my fears, and hit send. I finally did something that had stopped me so many times over for so many different reasons. I sent my book to the publishing house I had been working with for over two years, Balboa Press, a division of Hay House.

When I was looking through your website, I instantly felt, "He gets it! He sees the beauty in a letter that I feel in my heart every time I write one." Once I saw your website, I heard, "Move forward even though you have been discouraged over this project. It will be even better than you originally imagined."

You see, my book's working title, as I have submitted to Balboa Press, is *From Heart to Hand: The Lost Art of a Written Letter.* It is a compilation of letters I have written to people I love, individuals who inspire me, and those whose stories have touched me, whether I know them personally or not. The letters thank them for inspiring me and sharing their stories in such a vulnerable way. I wrote this book because I love writing letters, and I just believe that so much can come from this project. I want to be a part of reviving this lost art of a written letter, but I have been stalled with it many times over for so many different reasons. And these reasons are becoming quite clear in this moment.

So just over a month ago, I got my initial evaluation back from my check-in coordinator, and the e-mail discouraged me. I now know I was choosing to be discouraged even after the encouraging phone conversation I had with my coordinator. How I choose to look at it today is that everything happens in divine order, and even though it might take more work than I expected, I will finish my book.

Alex, I got something I wasn't even aware that I was looking for, to the point where I don't even know that I could put it all in words right now that would do it justice. I have received an unexpected rejuvenation of spirit. Your work is truly amazing, and I feel extremely blessed to have found it. So thank you for what you do, and thank you for this surge of unexpected inspiration that I have received from you. I do believe that several hands have played a role in this, not only our earth angels but a very special angel in heaven now. And I feel that in every part of my being. So thank you, thank you, thank you.

From my heart and hand to yours,
Kristin Horvath

Chapter 4
A Onetime Meeting Is Sometimes All It Takes

A Powerful Impact: An Angel

Dear Bill,

I write you this letter today from a place at the bottom of my heart. Bill, I know I only met you once, but you are the type of person who makes an impact in people's lives, and you had an effect on me when I met you. I will think of that night with Judy, Doug, you, and myself at the Bob Seger concert with such fond memories, joy, laughter, and happiness. It was a great night, and I felt blessed that evening that I had met both you and Judy. In those few hours we spent together, I took away that you are a man who is kind, caring, loving, compassionate, giving, and very loyal to the people in your life. And that combination of characteristics are such admirable qualities, and I am thankful to have met you that night and to be able to see all the love that is in your heart for the people who surround you.

I just wanted to let you know my thoughts and prayers are with you and Judy as they have been from the day I met you, and they always will continue to be. Thank you so much for the beautiful positive impact you had on me. It takes a very special person for that to happen to me, and I will forever be grateful and always remember these qualities as how I want to be in my life and how I want others to be toward my son and me.

If there is anything I can do to help either you or Judy, please don't hesitate to contact me at any time. Prayers and blessing to you, Bill. You are loved.

Kristin Horvath

★ ★ ★

I stopped everything I was doing on the day I received a text message saying that Bill had just been diagnosed as terminal and only had a short time here on this earth before he transitioned. It became instantly very important to me to get out everything I had to say so he knew the beautiful impact he had on my life. I had so much respect for Bill when I heard the story of the relationship between him and his son Phil. As I was told, Phil was not Bill's biological son. Bill had dated Phil's mother many years ago, and when the relationship ended between the two of them, Bill still wanted to continue to play a role in Phil's life, and he did with all of his love through his dying days until the very end of his life.

Within two weeks of mailing Bill's letter to him, I received the information that Bill had passed, and for a moment I wondered if he got the chance to read my words. I said some prayers and held thoughts of him and his family in my heart. I was sent me a text message shortly after I received the sad news, asking if I could come to Bill's funeral. I let them know I would absolutely be there. In the message I also learned that they had received and read my letter and it had touched them deeply.

The funeral mass was a beautiful celebration of Bill's life and a testament to the wonderful man I had met just that one time. After the service, everyone gathered in the church and stood in the receiving line to give our condolences to Bill's wife and family. When it came to be my turn, I could feel the tears well up in the back of my eyes. I blinked them away, not wanting to let them out right there. I took a quick breath and approached Judy. She reached out both of her hands toward me and said my name three times. And we stood there and held each other.

She said, "I wanted you to know that, when we received your letter, we read it over and over. He was so touched. We were all so touched by your words, and it couldn't have come into his life at a better time. It raised his spirits, and we surrounded ourselves around it. It helped put all of us in such a beautiful place."

Judy also let me know that pretty much every single one of their friends who were there that day had read the letter, and they all just wanted to thank me for the beautiful gift I had been able to give them in the last moments of Bill's life. This is one of the most touching moments I've had in reference to a letter I had written to someone, and I will hold onto thoughts of Bill and his family for many years to come. I am blessed to have such a wonderful angel in my life now.

Don't Give Up

Dear Phil,

This letter finds its way to you from the kindness of my heart. Doug texted me out of the blue on Friday night and gave me a little information as to what the current circumstances are with your health, and I wanted to reach out to you. You know you are going to be just fine. I feel it in my heart, and I hope you do as well. I am sure, when you look at your beautiful girls and lovely wife, you feel their love and your love for them and know that what you are going through right now are just your current circumstances. It is something you have to go through for some reason, and I want you to remember, as you do, that it doesn't define you. But you can define what this is and what this will be, and you have a lot of life left to live.

One of my initial thoughts when I read Doug's text was that you have some of the most incredible angels up there looking over you (one you know I have a particular fondness, admiration, and love in my heart for, Bill) protecting you and your family, and they are making sure you remember to just breathe your way through this. If you listen closely, I am sure you can hear them in your thoughts, telling you that you will be fine. And they are reminding you to fill your heart with the love that surrounds you, and they are advising you to let go of any and all worry.

I also wanted to reach out to you to share the names of some pretty amazing people I have been researching and studying for the past several years who specialize in the power of positive thoughts and affirmations. A little positive thought goes a long way and can never hurt anyone, so if you are open to this, I would suggest you look into Louise Hay and her book, *You Can Heal Your Life*. It is an amazing piece of work, and there is also a movie about it that you can get on DVD. I highly recommend watching it when you're ready.

We all have healing to do in our lives, whether it is learning how to forgive or love ourselves more or letting go of negative past circumstances that somehow seem to creep into our thought process. This book just seems to help in times when people have needed it the most in their lives, so I hope you will go online and buy yourself a copy or have Tammy do it for you.

Another great person to look into, whose messages about life I just love listening to, is Dr. Wayne Dyer. He is actually originally from Michigan, the east side of Detroit, the Mt. Clemens area. Go on YouTube and watch some of his videos. They have the potential to help with the mental battle and game you may be playing with yourself about everything that is going on in your life and all that has happened to you this year.

I am going to make just one more suggestion for now. You and Tammy should go look at hayhouse.com. On the left side, you can click on newsletters. Look at those, and see what resonates with you. It is free to subscribe to any or all of them. Louise Hay, Dr. Wayne Dyer, and Gregg Braden all had cancer of one form or another. They believed, and they all talk about their illnesses in their own way and how the power of positive thought helped get them through it.

Also on the hayhouse.com site, up at the top toward the left, click on hay house radio. It will take you to their online radio station, and on the left-hand side, you will see show hosts. Click on that, and you will get an amazing list of people to look into. More importantly, some have had similar experiences to what you are going through, so it is a way of knowing you are not alone and hearing what helped them that may be able to help you.

Phil, I hope I haven't overstepped my boundaries with this letter. I think you know how I felt about Bill, and I just wanted to let you know your entire family will hold a special place in my heart. You truly are lovely people, and you are a good friend to Doug, something I really appreciated. One can never have enough good friends in his or her life, so you need to stick around to be that good friend to him, a great husband to your wife, and the incredible father you are to those beautiful little girls, as I know you want to. Just remember to breathe. You will be fine.

I hope that maybe there was just one thing said in this letter that will help. You are in my thoughts and prayers. Give Tammy my best and Judy too.

From my heart to my hand for you,
Kristin

A Night at the Ballpark

Hi, Terry. I hope this e-mail finds you and your family well and your travels back home were safe and enjoyable. It was so nice talking with all of you that evening at Comerica Park, and please give your wife my sincerest apologies for spilling the beer down her back. I hope you and Sherry enjoyed your visit to Detroit and our city and suburbs treated you well. There really is a lot to see and do around this beautiful state of ours. The next time you visit, I suggest you take the family up north to Harbor Springs, Petoskey, or Traverse City and visit some of the wineries. Black Star Farms is my favorite place to stay.

In conversation with you, it was so wonderful to see the adoration you still have for your wife after thirty-plus years. (My parents were married for almost fifty years before my father passed away). I could see the love you have for your children and are able to enjoy in their successes with them. I truly hope your year ahead has many blessing for all of you. Again it was a pleasure sitting and talking with you at the Tigers game. Have a great rest of the week.

Kristin Horvath

★ ★ ★

I got such a great response from Terry and Sherry. I love when I meet total strangers and feel like we are kindred spirits once we start talking. And we can just go on and on for hours without a struggle. I have thought of the Friedman family many times since I met them, and I've had nothing but kind thoughts and blessings for them in all their life endeavors. It is situations like these that I love to hold onto because, when you're having a rough day or go of things, I can just think of these beautiful moments with complete strangers, and it helps my energy raise to a better place.

You Never Know What Will Happen
When You Sit Next to a Stranger

Dear Mike,

I don't know if you remember me, but we met about two months ago when I was at the Hamlin Pub. You were enjoying a night out while your wife was competing in a horse competition that weekend. I have been meaning to sit and take a minute to e-mail you several times over the past two months for a couple reasons. First, I want to say how much I enjoyed meeting you and conversing with you that evening. I loved talking photography and steadicams, but most of all, I really appreciated your input and insight into my passion project of writing a book. Your general curiosity about what I was doing in taking the time to write letters to individuals who have inspired me to thank them reignited the flame inside me that had been temporarily put out. It gave me a sense of excitement again that I had allowed to be sucked out of me to such a point where I made some instant changes in my life that weekend. I took some time for me and went down to Nashville for a week. (I also want to learn how to write country music lyrics.) I came back, and I have been rebuilding my purpose since then.

I wanted to thank you for your opinions and advice on starting a blog with the theory behind it being the blog will write the book. And thank you just for your kindness that evening. It is not often we find people who have a general appreciation in hearing about others following their passions, and you did. It is in those times when the naysayers come along that I will think of you and individuals like you who seem to understand what it is for someone to follow a passion and take the time to offer pieces of advice so I can get that much closer to completing something I love to do. I have bought my domain name for my website blog, and now I just need to find some help from the kindness of someone's heart to help me build it. Having been a chef isn't conducive to keeping up with the technological standards out there today, but I am learning. The name of the website is letters2share.com, and as soon as I get that help, I am looking forward to get it up and running. I will let you know, and you will definitely be able to look at it and say, "I had a part in that."

Thank you again. I am truly grateful you were put in my path that night. Hope all is well with you, and I hope that your wife and her horse did well that weekend.

Cheers,
Kristin A. Horvath

★ ★ ★

I don't know what I love more about this story: the fact I had such an aha moment when I was talking to a complete stranger about what I was doing or Mike's response that he really remembered the specifics of what I told him about my son and how much he loved the steadicam work he had done. He then referenced articles and videos for my son to look at. To have that feeling that a complete stranger wants to see you succeed in following your passions is so beautiful.

Mike was one of the nicest, sincerest men who took an honest interest in our conversation, and you just always seem to remember people like that. I did send my son all the information that Mike had sent me after I contacted him, and my son thought it was nice that a complete stranger was taking an interest and wanted to share some information with him. I know now that the information that Mike provided for my website/blog will be very helpful once I get ready to face my fears with certain technology (like creating my own website) and turn it into a curiosity instead of a fear.

I could just feel that evening that this complete stranger wanted nothing more for my son and me to completely succeed in following our passions. I also know that I will keep him posted along the way so he knows how a onetime meeting can have such a nice impact on someone's life.

A Helping Hand

Nick,

This is way overdue—and I apologize for that—but I just wanted to take a second to write a quick thank-you note to say how grateful I was that you took time out of your busy schedule to come over and help guide Christopher with his future endeavors. I also wanted to keep you posted with his status.

He has been accepted into film school at Full Sail University. He is getting everything all into place, and we will be leaving next month, moving him to Winter Park, Florida. He will be starting classes at the end of March. He is very excited, and as I am sure you know, I am thankful he is not moving to Los Angeles just yet. Florida seems to be more accessible than California, and as hard as it is going to be for me to see him go, I am glad this is where he has chosen to pursue his passion.

Anyway I hope all is going well with your thesis. It was a pleasure to meet you and your mother, and thanks again for sharing your experiences and insight with Christopher. I think it definitely got him in the right frame of mind and sent him on the right direction. Take care and have a great weekend.

Kristin

★ ★ ★

Anytime someone helps my son, it is extremely important for me to take a second and let him or her know how much it meant.

An Instant Bond

Dear William,

Happy anniversary! I know that sounds a little weird seeing as we are not dating and have only met each other once. A year ago, our dear friends got married, and we met at their wedding, which was a tad bit of fun to say the least. Since then and more recently than anything, you have been an absolute peach. No, not just because you live in Georgia, silly, but mostly because you put up with me. I truly appreciate that you are very entertaining with your witty comments and quick one-liners with your text messages and Facebook posts. You take my calls and return my texts anytime under any conditions, no matter how I am feeling, and you always have a great response for me. And for all this, I am truly grateful that I met you. Don't change not for a second who you are, and I can only be so lucky to have you in my life as a friend for a long time to come.

Thank you for being you. I am grateful I know you, and I just wanted to tell you.

Love,
Kristin

I do believe that God works in mysterious ways and he brings people together to help each other. William and I have stayed friends, and we call or text a few times a year to see how things are with each other. He checks in to see how my writing is going since he knows it is what I love to do, which is so nice of him.

After I had received a message with Christmas blessings, I decided to write another quick letter.

I would have never known myself that night we met that we would have had the bond we share now, and when I sent you that letter a year after we met and didn't hear from you until you told me what you had been going through and the road you had ahead, I knew I wanted to be there to support you and send you good thoughts and positivity. You shared your vulnerability with me, and once someone shows me that, I will always treat him or her with love and respect. You helped remind me of that, and I thank you.

You know, William, I love that we check in with each other a couple times a year, which just comes from a place of complete respect and happiness for each other. That is a beautiful thing. We never know how we are going to impact one's life whose path we come across. When treated with kindness, we become a person who can welcome someone on our path at any point, and it usually seems to be the right timing when our paths do cross. I will always keep you posted, and I ask you do the same for me. Here is to a life filled with love, joy, and happiness. Cheers, my friend, and always stay in touch.

Kristin

Chapter 5

Letters That Deserve
Their Own Chapter

When He Needed It the Most

Dear Mr. Sullivan,

This letter is many years overdue, but I guess it can fall under that "better late than never" pile in life. As I follow my passions in life, which I finally began to do the year after my father passed away, I have found myself over the past two years writing letters with thoughts of gratitude to those who have inspired me throughout my life and individuals for whom I am thankful to have in my life for the help they have given me. Not only do I do this because of the love I have for writing; it's also simply because I feel it is very important to let those individuals know the positive impact they've had on me.

This letter finds its way to you as both a thank you for your kind and gentle spirit you have always shown anytime our paths have crossed and a thank you for the experiences you gave my son when he was a young boy. (I am sure he will always remember his first private airplane ride.) Most of all, this letter serves as a thank you for all those great memories you and my father shared together. A lot of the stories of his college days (and he shared so many of them with me, especially since I attended his alma mater) seemed to include your name. I cherish the fact that I was able to walk the same hallways, sit in the same classrooms, and even have one of the same teachers my freshman year that my father had his senior year for ethics, Fr. Meuller.

More importantly I want to thank you for the most important time in my father's life you spent with him, and that was in the hospital during his last days. You showed him such love just by showing up. You allowed him to laugh, reminisce, and reflect upon his life with such bright memories of a friendships that spanned over fifty years. One could only be so lucky to have a friend like you in his life for such a long time. Thank you for that continued joy you gave him in his final days, and I am so grateful to have been there to reminisce, laugh, and relive so many of the memories you both had shared together.

I learned many things from my father, as I am sure you could understand, but one thing he instilled in me not just from his words but also by his actions was loyalty to his work, his family, and his friends. I am so grateful he had such a strong sense about him when it came to those things that were important to him.

As I sit and reflect for a minute, I remember a few years back when my mother and I ran into you, your wife, and your friends on New Year's Eve. What a wonderful surprise that was, and what an even lovelier conversation we had that I will always remember. The way in which you spoke of my father with such enduring admiration and sincerity was just what my mother and I needed that evening. I know from how he always spoke of you that it was such a mutual admiration, and I can't help but think he had a hand in bringing us together that evening just to give us all a little extra smile.

Thank you for being such a good friend to my father, especially when he needed it the most.

Sincerely,

Kristin A. Horvath

★ ★ ★

I am so glad I reached out to Mr. Sullivan. It's my way of keeping the beautiful memories of my father close to my heart.

★ ★ ★

The Lost Moon: Live with No Regrets

Dear Captain Lovell,

I write you this note for two reasons. You see, I have recently discovered that one can undo regrets he or she may have had in his or her life in order to eliminate living his or her life with remorse. With that said, I am attempting to undo a regret I've had since the mid to late nineties. I was working for the University of Detroit Mercy (my alma mater as well), and you were coming to campus for a meet-and-greet lecture series, and I had every intention to walk across campus to meet with you and have you sign my copy of your book, *Lost Moon*, and to tell you of my father (now deceased) and how he designed the nose cone to one of the Redstone missiles. He was a University of Detroit and University of Michigan grad, and he worked almost forty years for Chrysler Corporation. And part of that time in the sixties and seventies, he worked for Chrysler's missile division. With my head buried in my work the evening you were on campus, time got away from me, and I never made it across campus to meet you like I had wanted to.

The other night, my son, my mother, and I sat and started watching HBO's miniseries with Tom Hanks as the executive producer and narrator, *From Earth to the Moon*. And so many different emotions came rushing back to me, from my father's accomplishments with the space program (which I know so little about) to the regret of never having met with you when I had the opportunity.

I also write this letter to do what I meant to accomplish so many years ago, to say thank you for all you did with your career as an astronaut. "Amazing" is the first word that comes to mind to this day whenever I hear the stories of what you accomplished and the role you played in our nation's quest of space exploration. I know this might seem silly, but I truly wanted to take the time out of my day to thank you for all the history you made. My family gets so much joy to this day out of hearing about it and watching it. We relive it through stories that we share close to our hearts, and for this I am truly grateful.

Your book, *Lost Moon*, still sits by my bedside to this day. I wish you and your family the best in 2011.

Sincerely,
Kristin A. Horwath

★ ★ ★

Kristin Horvath

I loved going to the Dentist

Dear Dr. Sutherland,

It is with thoughts of love, friendship, kindness, and compassion that this letter finds its way to you today. For some time, I have been saying to myself that I want to sit and write you a letter, thanking you for being such a great dentist to my whole family for twenty-plus years. But more importantly I have wanted to write you to thank you for all the heartfelt kindness you have given us throughout the years and always taking a genuine interest in our lives. You have shared in the joys, sorrows, and accomplishments we have all had, and you especially took a genuine interest in Christopher. Because of you, going to the dentist was something we never dreaded but always looked forward to. It has always been so nice getting caught up with you and Colleen and sharing the stories of our families. In fact it is something I look forward to when I make my appointment.

There are reasons why we put off doing certain things that we feel in our heart, and sometimes we completely understand why. And other times we just accept it as being in the divine order that it was meant to be in. After our conversation today, I knew exactly why I had not written you, and that is because you need to hear now, more than at any other point in your life, about what an incredible person you are. You need to remember the man who once existed without question or thought, living life wholeheartedly every day when he woke up, is still there. I know I am speaking very honestly here, but that is because it comes from my heart and I think you are open and ready to hear such honesty. It was such an honest and vulnerable conversation you had with me today.

I can't imagine what you are going through. I am not trying to pretend I know exactly how you feel, but I do know that I might just be able to say one thing. I might be able to give you one piece of information that you need to see, hear, or read that will help you get back to the man I have come to know and admire for so many years. I do firmly believe your life will be greater than it is today and greater than it ever has been before.

I think, because of the simple fact of how you engaged in conversation with me yesterday in an honest and wholehearted way about where you are at this point of your life, you do have a willingness to be open to hearing new things that will help you to feel happier and healthier in no time. You were so receptive to hearing about Louise Hay and her book, *You Can Heal Your Life*, so I hope you do order it because so much good information is in there that you can benefit from it. I literally just finished writing this sentence when your assistant Colleen called me this morning to give me your e-mail address. She told me that you went online last night and you had already ordered it and started reading it. I was so touched when she told me about this and your openness to hear what I had to say.

I am so grateful that I was able to give you an incredible resource through all the research, reading, and studying I have been doing myself over the past several years. I would like to also suggest that you go to her website, www.louisehay.com, and subscribe to her newsletter. And go to www.drwaynedyer. com and subscribe to his newsletter as well. He has some of the most amazing things to say that I really think you will be able to grasp onto them. I have already forwarded his latest newsletter, which just came out yesterday, to your e-mail, so I hope you were able to read it. Also go to YouTube to look up both of them and watch their videos. This is a great thing for you to do in your down-time now. Watch them more than once because you will get something different out of it every time you do. Go buy yourself a new notebook, and write down the things that resonate for you. This will help lift you into a more positive direction. You know how I feel about writing, so do this one for me. Writing can be so healing for the soul.

I do believe that what you think you create. So if thoughts come into your mind that are negative or defeatist, all you simply have to do is change the channel to a happier one. I do also want to say that one thing I did hear in our conversation yesterday, which was probably the most important thing that I could have heard, was how grateful and thankful you were that your job required you to sit most of the time. Even though you have had to cut back on your hours, you were still able to go to work, and you knew you were blessed because of that. I recognized that thought process was a great step in the right direction. Having thoughts of thanks and gratitude always is, and it was so good to hear you say it.

I want to thank you for being a part of my life's journey; being open and willing to hear the things I have to share; always being so kind, gentle, and understanding; and allowing me to have a payment plan over the years when insurance didn't cover things. None of this was ever lost on me, and I am so grateful that I can now give back a little to you.

If you ever want to share your progress, because there will be advancement, I would be more than glad to hear about it. Also one more resource I wanted to give you, which I also gave to Colleen yesterday, is www.hayhouseradio.com. They have a lot of great speakers on there, and as Louise herself would say, "You can hear the same thing being said by fifteen different people and not get it, but when one particular person says it, sometimes it just resonates better for someone." So I would suggest you explore all of the wonderful people on there and see if anyone just really clicks with you. When you are ready, there are a bunch of people on Facebook whose posts I like to read, so you can go onto my page. (I have just requested you as a friend.) And you can see who my likes are, such as Sunny Dawn Johnson or Mary Morrissey. Take a look at their pages. Explore and see what feels right for you.

You know I am wishing the best thoughts out there for you.

From heart to hand just for you,
Kristin A. Horvath

My Domain Name Was Born

Dear Joshua,

Do you believe in signs? I do, and tonight I received one. I had been working on trying to come up with a domain name all day for a website blog spot I want to create, all with little success. Then my roommate came home and was telling me about her day. She said they had a wonderful motivational speaker at work who came to speak with two of the teams on campus and how great it was for the girls. I decided to pull up your website and started looking around. I realize I had already been on your site once before, but tonight I saw something different. I saw a potential for me to grow.

As I was talking to my roommate about what I had been trying to do all day to come up with a domain name and saying I definitely wanted the word "letters" in it, we started throwing around ideas, and she suggested "the art of lost letters." And my mind started going with that. I looked at my roommate and said, "Yes, that is how I started this project, and it is going to be a part of this, but it has evolved into more than just that."

Then as I was looking at your website, it rolled off my tongue, and as it did, chills came over my body. I wrote down "letters2share.com." I showed it to my roommate, and my domain name was born and purchased. It was a wonderful moment, and I just wanted to say thank you for the unexpected inspiration.

Kristin

My Longest Relationship: My Hairdresser

Dear Bill,

I just want to take a second to sit and write to tell you how very dear you are to me. I know I may only get a chance to see you about four or five times a year, but I wanted to tell you how much I look forward to those visits, as I like to call them, instead of appointments. To this day, every time I walk into your salon, I can take a deep breath and relax. I can't remember exactly when you first started doing my hair, but I know it was sometime around 1993. Oh my gosh! Almost twenty years! I laugh when I think about how you are one of my longest, most consistent relationships I've had. I may have strayed a time or two or gone to the store to buy a box of color, but you were always there when I would come back. I always came back, and you would fix the havoc I had unleashed on my hair. And for that I am truly grateful.

It has been an absolute privilege to watch your life over the past twenty years, from opening up your own salon, opening an even bigger business, walking away from it all after wanting to pursue a corporate career, and realizing where your real happiness was, the adoption of your son Louise, who has had the most incredible impact on you. The things we do for our kids! You decided to come back to your roots and thankfully mine too (some pun intended), and you gracefully settled back into a one-man salon so you could build your schedule around your beautiful son.

Fatherhood suits you like nothing else I've seen in your life. We have seen different relationships come and go in our lives, and some stick around way more than we ever wanted. We've seen friendships come and go, and we were sad to let go of some, but fond memories are shared of them. We have imparted so many intimate conversations that I truly feel a bond with you because of this. You are someone I have never had to hold back my thoughts with, and that is because you don't judge me. After all these years, I do believe you get me, where I have been, where I am now, and where I want to go. You understand one of the most important things in life, aside from our children, and that is how important it is to have thoughts of gratitude and giving thanks. And it is such a beautiful quality for you to have.

Bill, I could seriously sit and write for hours all the stories we have shared with each other over the twenty years, like the time I was growing out my hair and I came into the salon with my hair pulled back in a low neck ponytail. You asked me, as you always did, if I were ready to cut it off, and I said, "Yeah, maybe." And with a swift movement of the scissors, you took the ponytail right off and then poured me a glass of wine to help alleviate the shock of it all. And you gave me a beautiful short haircut that I adapted to for a few years. That story still makes me laugh.

I also love how, every time I come in for my appointment, you have to ask me which side I part my hair on, and we both start laughing. I know that will always be an ongoing joke with us.

I also wanted to tell you how glad I was that I was in the salon the day of my last visit. What I saw was you finally getting the closure you needed and deserved. Now it's time to celebrate your life. We go through things for reasons, so we can better understand ourselves and continue to grow in life. Now that chapter of your life is closed. I look so forward to hearing about your future and sharing all of our stories of life's journey every three months for the next twenty years.

You are a very dear person in my life, and I couldn't be luckier to have you as my hairstylist for as long as I have. I am truly grateful for so much that you have given me over the years, from your advice to just listening, free products, discounted services in tough times, and sharing your journey with me as well. You are a wonderful and beautiful kindred spirit. I hope the holidays were good to you and Louise and all your dreams come true in the New Year.

Love,
Kristin Horvath

PS. Here is to my dream that one day you will do my hair for my wedding.

★ ★ ★

I sent this next letter to those people who touched my life the first week I arrived in Nashville on March 30, 2014, with just me, my car, and all my belongings in a sixteen-foot Penske truck.

My New City, My New Home:
My First Week in Nashville

Karen, Lori, Harry, Shawn, and Karyn,
My first week somewhere new,
I will always remember this time and how I grew.
Blessed with friends and blessed with love,
Nashville and me fit like a hand in a glove,
The humbleness in a stranger who became a new friend.
The words in a performance helped me to mend.
The kindness in the few people I knew my first week in
 Nashville, I will always remember this time and how
 I grew.
The mountains that surround me have made me whole.
The inspiration you see in others has filled my soul,
The light in someone's eyes when they talk about their dreams.
Life down here is just as it seems,
The comfort I have embraced so quickly in this town I
 now call home.
I can look beyond my first week in Nashville now
And see how I will grow.
Your presence in my life lifted me so I never felt alone.
You touched me in a way that was gentle and kind,
Like a guardian angel telling me everything will be just fine.
So I thank you for the smile, the hug, the kindness, and the
 joy you gave to me that you might not even have known.
But because of you, my first week in Nashville I will always
 remember.
I planted my roots, and you helped them to grow.

With love and gratitude,
Kristin

Chapter 6

Letters from Others

Do you have any letters that you have held onto over the years, either tucked away in some box in your closet or in a drawer you haven't opened for a while? I know I have a box or two of letters I have held onto, and I will occasionally pull out a few and reminisce. I would love to know whose letters you have held onto. If you may be so inclined to share any of your letters, you may go to www.letters2share.com and tell us about them.

My Aunt Adele and Uncle Bill shared the following letter. My Uncle Mike (my mother's brother) wrote the letter to his wife, my Aunt Marilyn, and it is one of the most beautiful love letters I have ever seen.

A True Love Letter

My darling Marilyn,

Thirty-eight years ago, so much happened. So little happened. For me it has been an incredible journey of love filled with joys, beauty, passion, trials, sacrifices, pain, happiness, challenges, and peace. The stuff of life. The good life, the hard life, the quiet life, and the disquieting life. The travails, the turmoil, the lust for life, our life, our togetherness, our love, and mostly our love.

Yet so little happened. Wasn't it only yesterday, August 10, 1957, when we married? Wasn't it only yesterday when we drove to Harbor Springs, Michigan, for our honeymoon? I think perhaps it was yesterday. But our lives together began even before that.

I still see you quite clearly standing by yourself with your arms folded across a light blue blouse you wore, standing there waiting. The music played, and we danced the dance of life, the stuff that fires up the soul, and the stuff that smolders and causes smoke and then a raging fire, the stuff of our lives. How we began for me, that is how it is today. So little has happened to change that. So much has happened to enlarge that, a hill that became a mountain. I know how it is for God when God changes hills into mountains. What joy! What utter joy.

Then the new lives appeared. We shared in all those moments of bliss before those seven wonders appeared. It was always bliss, sheer bliss. The seven wonders came with our love. God's too. Clearly each was born with the sign of love and peace over them and in them. Our blessings were upon them. God's in them. That will never change. Grow, yes; change, never. Each arrived with his mother bearing the pain and joy of their arrivals; their father had the awe of it all, especially the awe of creation and the courage of the mother. It was awesome each time. I hold you in awe, the mother of our children.

Your sacrifices, your pains, sorrow, and even lamentations, I feel them all. Awesome. You're something else. You bore it all. You, the unique, beautiful, and inspiring woman who made it all happen with the likes of me at your side.

I thank you. No, I deeply thank you for all you have done for your love, first and foremost, your sacrifices, your tenderness, your compassion, and your mercy. You are my fountain of life. Thank you for the daily sustenance you give me, yourself. Thank you for the joy you put into my life, our life. May God love my wife divinely forever. I know I will. Thank you, Lord, for Marilyn. I love you. I love you. I love you.

Mike

★ ★ ★

It helps to have a family member as a priest who can put his perspective on grief. I have held onto the following letter for just over ten years now. One of my father's relatives sent it to my mother a few months after my father passed.

A Beautiful Perspective on Grief

July 22, 2005

Dear Shirley,

Please accept my condolences to you and your family upon the death of your beloved husband and to his children. We all have experienced that death of our beloved parents, sisters, brothers, in-laws, and friends. We both know the list. I still have some vivid remembrances about the Horvath (John and Catherine) family. I remember visiting them many years ago in Detroit and admiring the Horvath boys. Our lives are full of pleasant, happy, and sorrowful memories. I also recall some visits with you and Bob, but I can't remember I have a presumption that it was at the funerals of Catherine and John. May they, Bob, and all our beloved deceased rest in the love and peace of our Lord and Savior Jesus Christ.

Your funeral musical part must have been very beautiful. The thoughts contained in those selections were inspiring. I hope you keep the thoughts and aspirations in those prayers in your heart and minds. You will find the consolations, faith, and hope in those thoughts. You and your family certainly suffered together with Bob. May you support each other in your daily prayers and lives. May Jesus welcome Bob's soul into heaven, and may we all meet there happily one day. The realization of our own death leads us to think about the purpose of our lives according to God's plans for us.

Thank you for your mass intentions for Bob. I will say the first mass for the repose of his soul this Sunday, July 24. A few days ago, I received a letter from Dorothy Kish asking masses for the living and deceased of the Kish, Stevens, and Horvath families. I know you two keep in touch with one another. I am happy to know that.

May Bob's ashes rest in peace whether in Michigan or the Grand Tetons. God has created many most wonderful things like the Tetons and all the marvels of his creation, and he created all this earthly and planetary wonders and beauty for our needs to be astonished of his creation and thankful for his love for us, the human family.

Keep on living your God-given life in the faith, hope, and love of Christ. May Christ's holy mother, the Virgin Mary, bless you and yours all the days of your life. Have a true devotion to her.

With prayerful best wishes and in the love of Christ,

Fr. M Kish

I have held onto this letter because of the stories I heard while growing up about the Kish (my father's mother's side) family and in particular Fr. Kish himself. My mother corresponded with Fr. Kish for years. I also have the Bible that Fr. Kish gave to my father on his graduation from high school, and my parents also used it on their wedding day at mass. The inscription reads:

To Bob:

On the occasion of his graduation from high school in the year of Our Lord 1948.
    Knowledge gained from secular source are valuable tools but the knowledge within this book is a tool of insurmountable value. For it is a tool and a key for this life and the one to come.

Fr. Matthew Kish

I love that I have these beautiful pieces, and I will hand down my father's Bible to my son one day.

★ ★ ★

This next letter was written to me in 1991. I carried it with me every day in my backpack during college. The envelope is in pieces, and the letter itself is now actually in two pieces from the amount of times I took it out of my backpack and read it. I felt then as I still do today like the most amazing blessings were bestowed upon me every time I read it.
    Brother Ignatius became a confidant and a friend to me when I was eighteen years old and pregnant. I would visit and

receive a Father Solanus blessing every time I visited, and we would walk the grounds of the monastery. He would share stories with me of his time with Father Solanus on the streets of Detroit. His words and stories were what I needed during that time in my life, and I am blessed to have had the bond with Brother Ignatius that I had.

After my son was born, it was very important to me that he was baptized at St. Bonaventure Monastery, where Brother Ignatius lived and where we had built our friendship, and to have Brother Ignatius present during the ceremony.

A Friar, My Friend

Dear Kristin,

What a pleasant surprise to receive your kind Easter greeting and note. Kristin, I deeply appreciate your thoughtfulness. I too often think of you and wonder how you are doing. So it was a joy to get your note and know you're keeping well and Christopher is a healthy and happy child. I'm happy to know you've gone back to college. Being a mom and a student is a big load to carry, but the fact that you're enjoying both sure makes it easier.

Kristin, I'd love to have a nice visit with you and also see and hug Christopher. Now that it's getting warmer, I hope you can manage to come for a visit soon. God bless.

Love and prayers,
Ignatius

* * *

I did go to see Brother Ignatius for the last time that spring, but unfortunately he was too ill to see me. So I asked for a pen and paper, and to this day I can remember sitting there and writing him a letter, telling him how much our friendship had and will always mean to me. I wish I had a copy of that letter today, but I am blessed to have had all the moments I did with such an unexpected friend.

This next and final letter of what has now become my first published book is from my father. He wrote it to me in 1988 when I was eighteen years old and I was attending my senior-year retreat. It is one of the most precious gifts I have ever received.

My Hero, My Mentor, My Best Friend:
A Letter to Me from My Father

My dearest Kristin,

During this time of contemplation, I'm sure you have thought about how your life will develop. What will you be? What will you do for a career? Where will you live? These are very important but not as important as your attitude toward these situations and developments. You are a happy person with a good positive attitude, and these characteristics will help make your life a happy one.

For you, I hope you develop persistence in seeing your goals. Determination is your greatest asset in achieving your goals. I think you know that persistence and determination can overcome many obstacles. Couple persistence with kindness, and you will never want for anything.

I hope you acquire all your material wants, a companion you want to spend your life with, a career that satisfies your mind, and a family you can love and be proud of. But most of all, I hope you can be proud of yourself. As you spend each day, spend it such that when you spend your last one, you look back, smile, and say, "I wouldn't change a thing." Above all, do this for yourself. The peace of mind and satisfaction will be worth the effort.

I want you to know I am proud of you. You have a pleasant personality and make friends easily. You have a good mind and can develop into anything you want to become. Effort is required, but I think you have learned this fact. Last of all, I want you to know I love you. Yes, I am a parent and must do the job of a parent. But I'll always love you because you're you.

Love,
Dad

★ ★ ★

To have this letter written on my old stationery and to see his words in his handwriting written for me is priceless.

My Dearest Kristen,

During this time of contemplation, I'm sure you have thought about how your life will develop. What will you be? What will you do as a career? Where will you live? These are very important, but not as important as your attitude toward these situations and developments. You are a happy person with a good positive attitude and these characteristics will help make your life a happy one.

For you I hope you develop persistence in seeking your goals. Determination to your greatest asset in achieving your goals. I think you know that persistence and determination can overcome many obstacles. Couple persistence with kindness and you will never want for anything.

I hope you acquire all your material wants, a companion you want to spend your life with, a career that satisfies your mind, and a family you can love and be proud of. But most of all I hope you can be proud of yourself. As you spend each day, spend it such that when you spend your last one you look back, smile, and say I wouldn't change a thing. Above all do this for yourself. The peace of mind and satisfaction will be worth the effort.

over

I want you to know I am proud of you. You have a pleasant personality and made friends easily. You have a good mind and can develop into anything you want to become. Effort is required but I think you have learned this fact. Last of all I want you to know I love you. Yes I am a parent and must do the job of a parent. But, I'll always love you because your you.

love,

Dad

One Last Thing

Dear readers,

I want to take a moment and say thank you for taking the time to read this book. I hope you have enjoyed some of the stories as I have enjoyed sharing them with you. This has been an incredible process and journey, and I have felt every emotion you can imagine over the several years it has taken me to finish this project. So from the bottom of my heart, it is filled with complete love as I let you know how grateful I am to have been able to share these honest, emotional, opinionated, and sometimes even compelling moments of my life with you through the letters I love to write.

From my heart and hand to yours,
Kristin

Who would you write a letter to?

Dear _____,

About the Author

Born and raised and having lived most of her life in the suburbs of Detroit, Kristin now resides in Nashville Tennessee and is an example of what it means to follow your passions. A graduate of the University of Detroit Mercy (Go Titans!) and a former Human Resources Manager, in 2006, Kristin decided to return to college and pursue her passion for cooking and became a chef.

Having a lifelong love for writing, Kristin has come out with this, her first book, *From Heart to Hand: The Lost Art of a Written Letter*, and is looking forward to seeing what things may come from it. As a single mother for twenty-seven years to her only child, Christopher, Kristin finds it very important to instill in him and others to do what you love, stay positive, and be grateful along the way, then everything will fall into place. ;)